D1495232

CHANGE
YOUR
THINK

AN UNEXPECTED WAY
TO THINK
ABOUT MANAGING PEOPLE

KRIS V. PLACHY, M.A.

ISBN-10   0983873607
ISBN-13   9780983873600
LCCN   2011935387

Book and cover designed by Ellie Searl

GRIZZLY PUBLICATIONS

El Dorado Hills, California

CHANGE YOUR THINK

This book is dedicated with love to the sweetest part of my life.
Mike, Ben, Kate, & Ian
Aujoo-boo

CONTENTS

"Praise the bridge that carried you over."
~ *George Colman*

INTRODUCTION AND ACKNOWLEDGMENTS

I've been coaching for over seventeen years. I didn't really know that's what I was doing for the first five years or so of my career. But in hindsight, I've come to realize that this profession chose me a long time ago. I found that I've been attracted to roles where I'm helping other people 'think' about their choices. Whether they've been personal or professional, I've been partnering with people as they navigate transitions and decisions in a variety of settings. My first position out of college set me up beautifully for this career: working with individuals as they decided whether or not to return to school to complete a degree. A decision that for some is so easy, while for others is tremendously difficult. Without this experience early in my career, I'm sure I would not be where I am today. I'll always be grateful to my good friend Clarissa for introducing me to the work. It was a gift that continues to give and give.

As I grew professionally, I stepped into management positions. The first management role I had was rough, to say the least. I bumped around like a blindfolded hot mess through that first year. It always seemed a shame to me that we don't prepare people better for management roles. It seems that we could make a better investment in our youth, to help them understand the demands of management. So, like many of you, I learned the hard way. I fell on my face more times than I care to count as a manager. I made little and not so little mistakes. But the advantage of falling down is you learn. Through that learning, I gained even more respect for coaching and the power of a strong coach.

As a young manager, I learned from colleagues like Bill and Heather, Ann and Vince. I learned that you can be held accountable with grace and love. I learned that coaching and leadership were inextricably tied to one another. As I advanced in my career, I also gained more and more access to the coaching profession. Through colleagues and mentors, I learned what true coaching and leadership looked like—that managing others could be a life changing, uplifting experience, not the day-to-day challenge that I experienced early in my career. My close friend and colleague Bob taught me how to keep things simple—how to be emotionally intelligent about people, without being 'emotional.'

I kept following the coaching path, which landed me square in front of Brooke Castillo. The day I met her, my life plan altered dramatically. Or it has happened exactly as it was supposed to. Regardless, Brooke's influence and wisdom has left a permanent impression and lasting impact on who I am as person, coach, and leader. I'm forever grateful for the day we met and the relationship that has ensued since.

I fostered enough confidence in my coaching skill to create a Performance Coaching team within an organization. Through a draft proposal for a coaching team, I found another ally and mentor. Trish is a woman of spirit and abundance. I'll never know anyone who has the kind of heart and demonstrates the level of advocacy as she. I've learned from Trish that being your team's best advocate is a hallmark of a strong leader. She is that and so much more.

The coaching team and I have navigated brilliant waters together. Kim, Heidi, Kate, Starla, Elisha, and Erin. We have learned together that what we teach, we must practice—that excellent coaches start with themselves, always. In order to teach others, we must embody the wisdom we espouse and we must live and breathe it. We have shared a journey few have the opportunity to have. For all of you, I'm grateful.

My learning has been in practice. Sure, I've read books, gone to school, etc. but the biggest lessons have been through application and testing. I've learned by watching amazing leaders who possess grace and inspiration. Dianne and Vicki, where would I be if not for the individual investment you've made in my growth. What you do is a lesson to us all. That to be a true leader, we must stop and take the time to pour into someone else. With authenticity and love, you both have done and continue to do so.

Becoming and being a great coach is a journey of self-discovery. It is a journey of the soul and I believe a reflection of the other spirits you allow into your life. The work I do is a natural outcome of the love I've received from my parents, my amazing husband Mike and our three kiddies, Ben, Kate, and Ian, and my dear friends Aimee and Jill. A coach is only as good as the playground for which he or she gets to practice and play on. For everyone whose lives have touched mine, I'll always be in your debt for allowing me the opportunity to learn alongside you.

A special and heartfelt thank you goes to Patricia Wick, who lovingly went through this entire book and edited and nudged me along the way.

This book is about sharing parts of my journey in the hopes that you can avoid some of the pitfalls that I or others have fallen into. Having the opportunity to lead a team is a gift. If handled with love and care, it can be a tremendous experience for everyone involved.

As you make your way through the book, you'll find space for several exercises. I encourage you to do the exercises as you read through the book. Having the practical application of your own examples will help you integrate the concepts more effectively.

I hope that you find the tools introduced in *Change Your Think* to be aligned with your own journey, and that they support you in your own growth as a coach, manager, and leader.

Kris

"It is the nature of thought to find its way into action."
~ *Christian Nevell Bovee*

1

WHO SHOULD READ *CHANGE YOUR THINK?*

W ho is this book for? This information included is for anyone who manages anybody. If you have employees, then this book is for you. It doesn't matter who your employees are. If they are line staff, directors or vice presidents. If you have a manager-employee relationship, then you will benefit greatly by applying the learning in this book. Why? Because as someone's manager you have intentionally or by complete accident, taken on the responsibility of developing someone's professional skills, abilities and behavior. In order to help someone improve their performance, you must understand them. You have to notice them and explore their thoughts, ideas, concerns. You, as a manager, are also someone's professional coach. Some of us get that, some of us think coaching is reserved for athletics. But I'm here to tell you, if someone works for you, you are their coach.

What does it mean to be someone's coach? There are certainly lots of definitions and descriptions out there. My favorite definition is offered by James Flaherty. He says that coaching or to coach is to help someone else understand the intention behind their behavior. If you apply this to the manager (as coach) employee relationship, my experience is that you find two distinct types. There are managers who do coach. They spend time and invest in understanding their employees' behavior and intention behind it. They learn more about their employees by asking good questions and listening. Then, there are managers who do not coach. They *tell*. They don't really invest in why their employees do what they do or don't do. They just want the work done. Arguably, this has been how most manager-employee relationships have operated. But the game is changing and employees expect more of their managers. Consequently, you'll need to expect more from yourself if you want to be a manager that can attract top talent, retain top talent and deliver successful results. You can help your organization go from here to there by expecting more from yourself as a coach. Your organization can move from where it is today to where it needs to go, by recognizing the same required advancement in your employees. Here, being their current abilities and skills to there, improved skill and performance.

One of the original uses of the word coach comes from "stagecoach." What did a stagecoach do? It brought its riders from where they are to where they want to go. Whichever way go employees, so to goes the organization. So, never underestimate the level of influence and impact you can have on each person who reports to you. That influence and impact is in direct correlation to how well you can coach your employees from where they are to where they want (and sometimes need) to go.

In organizations today, we seem to be working with three roles. We have leaders, managers and coaches. So what's the difference? In my view, it looks like this:

Leaders: Create vision and subsequently cultures where their team can thrive and succeed. They elevate the capacity of a group by motivation, inspiration, and modeling the behavior they expect. Often leaders are also in management roles, but that is not always the case. Many strong leaders never move into a traditional management position and many managers never acquire true leadership skill and capabilities.

Managers: Execute the leader vision. They reinforce policies and procedures. Managers support the goals of the organization by carrying out the implementation plans to achieve goals.

Coaches: Develop their team members. They observe skill and behavior. They provide feedback for improvement. Coaches help their team see how they can succeed or fail by their own action. They are ever present to reinforce learning through honesty, observation, and feedback.

So the question is, are these roles separate and distinct within an organization? Generally, no. A leader has to manage and a manager has to coach and a coach has to lead. For purposes of this book, we will reference you, the readers as a coach. You may not have coach in your title, but if you are in a management role, no matter what level within an organization, with people reporting to you, then you are a coach. As I mentioned earlier, when employees work for you, you have a responsibility as their coach to develop their abilities. The first part of this book actually won't be as much about them (your employees) as it will be about you. In order to become a brilliant, sought after and highly successful coach within your organization there is one person you must have a masterful coaching relationship with... can you guess who that may be? That'd be you. You must first be able to coach yourself before you can ever be a masterful coach.

What does that mean, coach myself? Have a conversation with myself? Talk out loud to myself? What? Well, when you are able to coach yourself you recognize that you are actually an active participant in whatever is going on around you. Most of us spend our time in a conversation with another person thinking about what *they* should do differently. We may think about what they should or should not have said. We may believe their actions should be different, etc. We focus entirely on the experience the other person is creating for us, rather than how we are choosing to respond to them. Coaches notice themselves in every encounter with another person or group. They notice what they are thinking, feeling and how they are responding to others. When I work with others, one of my favorite observations they inevitably make is, "Oh, if only my boss, co-worker, sister, parent could hear this." People instantly think about the context of their experience and see how someone *else* needs to benefit or change. They fail to see themselves in the experience and how they are contributing or participating to the overall outcome.

So, when I say that a good coach first must coach themselves, the first step is to recognize you are a player in every encounter you are involved in. As a result, you have something to notice about yourself and subsequently learn as a result. In the following chapters, we will apply the Self Coaching Model and see how the effects of 'seeing' yourself can lead to powerful results. Once you are capable of masterfully coaching yourself, it is amazing how you can then give that gift to others. The bottom line is, if you want to be recognized as an amazing coach, manager, or leader then take the time to learn the tools of this book. You will be transformed, your professional opportunities will blossom, and your team will thrive!

When you traditionally think about corporate coaching, you're most likely think of models for action, words to encourage and motivate, and powerful questions to drive understanding and awareness. Many corporate coaching tenets also reflect tools, techniques, and models utilized by sports coaches and athletic experts. This book is different. This book is about you as coach and how the thoughts that you believe about your team create and ultimately drive performance. The model applied within the context of this book is applicable to all coaching, however, as a manager-coach, your challenges are unique. So inside these chapters you will find examples related to common issues in the world of team management, leadership, and coaching.

"People who don't Think probably don't have Brains; rather, they have grey fluff that's blown into their heads by mistake."
~ Winnie the Pooh

2

WHAT IS *CHANGE YOUR THINK?*

E ver had an employee you can't stand? Drive you nuts? As a result, you learn and say swear words you thought would never roll off your tongue? Want to know why they bug you so badly? You're probably thinking it's because they are annoying, inept, or simply sent here to torture you. Actually, the real reason they are the bane of your existence has absolutely nothing to do with them and everything to do with your *thoughts* about them. Huh, you say? As you read this I can hear you spouting off all the reasons (known as evidence) you have to support your point. The employees in question (because you know there are more than one), are ignorant, they don't listen, they drone on, they interrupt, they brag, they're lazy, they... yeah, I get it. But here's what's really going on. Your employee does something (a circumstance or fact) and you create a thought about it. Where that becomes a major issue for you, is when you have subsequent bad feelings about it and you are short with them, yell at them, or even ignore them. When you are short with or yell at or ignore your employees, are you an effective coach? Probably not. The behavior that makes you crazy only gets worse, not better. But that's actually because you notice it more (there's that evidence thing again) because you are thinking more about it.

So basically, what I'm asserting is that challenging employee relationships are really your problem, not theirs. The good news is there is a path to a stress free management life. There is a method for learning how to deconstruct your thinking about your employees *before* you totally destruct the relationship between you.

Change Your Think is based on the model created by Brooke Castillo in her book *Self Coaching 101*. This coaching model will help you see how so much of the anguish that we face as leaders is literally fabricated. I'm sure it may be a bummer to realize that most of the stress, pain, and angst you've felt in your time as a manager has been based on stories of your mind. It's certainly much easier to make our pain someone else's fault. But truth be told (and we'll do a lot of that in this book), you've created your own pain by believing your own thoughts. Read on... your freedom from work-place angst awaits!

I've been a leader coach for a long time. I've led big teams, small teams, staff managers, and directors. There has always been a common theme to whatever level employee I've worked with, they're human, and so am I. That, however, is where the similarity ends. I've worked with passive employees, aggressive employees, funny and boring folks, eager and less than interested. I've had team members I'd invite to my home and those I've feared would ever know my address. So, trust me, I get that there are other humans on this planet who we believe are difficult, challenging and even scary. One thing remains true, for as long as someone is on your team, you are responsible to them as a manager and as a coach. You can maintain that role from a frustrated, unhealthy place or you can show up to them just as you do anyone else on your team, your choice. Circumstances do not determine your feelings about a situation or person, your thoughts do. And if you have to work with someone every day, might as well do so pain and stress free, don't you think?

So you may be thinking, "Am I supposed to ignore all the bad behavior and poor performance of employees on my team?" The short answer is absolutely not! Quite the contrary. When you get yourself out of the way, you actually are able to hold people more accountable. There is an entire section of this book dedicated to accountability. Believe it or not, most leaders struggle with accountability conversations. Because why? Because of their thoughts around accountability, that's why. More on that later. But what's true is that as a manager you are responsible for the performance and results of your team, division, region, etc. In order to maximize your team's ability to achieve results, you need to present a strong leadership and coaching presence. You achieve this presence by first having clarity around who you are, what you believe and how those 'stories' are impacting the team's ability to achieve peak productivity and results.

Change Your Think is about providing coaches who manage, a tool that will ALWAYS provide valuable insight into your decision-making, and the results you get from your players. Always! This book will put a refreshing spin and perspective on challenges that you have been externalizing and blaming others for, for some time. It will give you the opportunity to look at stories and thoughts that you believe are having an adverse impact on the outcomes you are getting. With the knowledge you will gain from this book, you will be a self-aware coach that leads from a place of objectivity and strength. When you lead with objectivity and clarity, you can support your team with their goals, their work, and their results. Everyone wins when you invest in yourself as a coach.

THE *SELF-COACHING 101* MODEL

Achieving self-awareness is where we will begin. We'll start by recognizing that we all have stories and experiences that make us uniquely who we are. A story is our version of life events.

For example:
- **I was born in Boston.**
- **Grew up in Puerto Rico.**
- **Ended up in California.**

Those are facts.

My story about this collection of facts is:
- **I was born in Boston, which in the few times I've been there is such an amazing town. It is so full of history and charm. I just love that I started my life there.**
- **Then my family and I moved to Puerto Rico. I was so fortunate to grow up living near the ocean and sailing with my parents. Living there gave me my love of the water and the passion I have for being as close to the beach as I can.**

We make our factual life experiences 'mean' something, by telling stories. Those stories are created when we add our thoughts to the facts. It is through those stories (collections of thoughts and beliefs) that we filter everything that goes on around us. As a manager, we bring those stories with us to our work. We bring them into our professional relationships and decision-making. The stories we have effect how and what we coach.

As a manager you encounter hundreds of issues, experiences, challenges, etc. every day in your work.

Let's take a moment for your first exercise.

Using the space provided, write down the top challenges you are currently having with managing or coaching individuals on your team.

1. _____

   _____

2. _____

   _____

3. _____

   _____

Now I want you tell me the story behind each of these challenges. Don't be shy. Tell the whole thing. Why are you having a challenge? What's going on?

_____

_____

_____

_____

_____

_____

_____

_____

_____

(continued)

_____

_____

_____

_____

_____

_____

We're going to come back to this information a little bit later on in this chapter.

There's no question that you constantly have to navigate choices and decisions. When you think about what you deal with, it's always best to approach your decision making and coaching perspective from a place of objectivity, at least as close to objective as possible. And while I know that many of you believe that you are very objective and are always using your 'thinking' brain, the reality of it is you are still using your 'story' filters to make your decisions and process information. There's nothing wrong with it, it just is what it is. Your thoughts about your life experiences inherently color how you view any new experiences that you have. As a manager, your awareness of these 'stories' helps you see how you are interacting with your staff. When it comes to coaching people, what you are using as a filter (through your stories) is where your work begins as a coach.

In the following section we will be breaking down the *Self-Coaching 101 Model* and how it applies to coaching employees. What you'll find in your review of this model is that it provides a simple, quick approach to gain better self-understanding in any situation.

THE *101 MODEL* WE WILL USE IN THIS BOOK IS AS FOLLOWS:

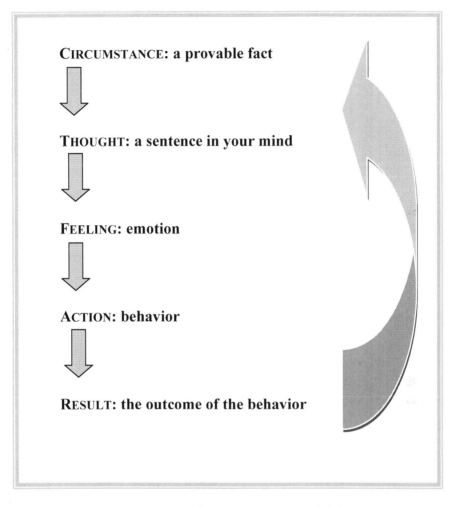

CIRCUMSTANCE: a provable fact

THOUGHT: a sentence in your mind

FEELING: emotion

ACTION: behavior

RESULT: the outcome of the behavior

Circumstances (facts) lead to thoughts, which create feelings. Those feelings inspire actions and behaviors, which ultimately lead to results. The results will always support the original thought. The thought wants to find evidence to support it. Simple enough right? Not terribly complex to see it on paper, but tremendously powerful when applied in action. In order to apply the *101 Model*, we first must explore each component and, of course, practice!

FACT FROM FICTION

One of the first steps to understanding the *101 Model* is to learn how to isolate facts (circumstances) from fiction (stories or thoughts we create in our mind). When we are used to believing our thoughts, we usually accept them as facts.

Here are some examples:
- **Jerry is lazy.**
- **Jerry is a non-performer.**
- **Lucy is obnoxious.**
- **Lucy doesn't listen.**
- **Larry is stubborn.**
- **Larry is disrespectful.**

If you are like most managers, as you read the list above, you inserted your own employees' names. And you could give lots of evidence to support your assertion that the employees are lazy, stubborn, disrespectful, and so on. "Those are facts," you'd say, "and I can prove them."

Let's try these examples:
- **Jerry did not complete a project.**
- **Jerry did not meet three out of five performance goals.**
- **Lucy asked me to repeat instructions two times today.**
- **Larry has not changed his position on our project.**
- **Larry rolled his eyes when I spoke today.**

Now, which of the two sets of examples are facts? Which ones would you have a better chance of proving in a court of law?

The first set of examples are actually someone's thoughts about a circumstance. Think about it. You are working with Jerry. He was supposed to finish a project by today and he didn't. You think to yourself "Ugh, there he goes again. That Jerry. He is so lazy!"

It's important for all of us to learn how to make the distinction between the facts about a situation and what we make those facts mean with our thoughts. As a coach, your job is to develop skill and behavior. A coach should work to develop employees based on observable patterns of behavior and challenges with skill development.

Your ability to isolate what is truly occurring, versus the thoughts you create, is the key to your successful coaching career.

Let's review another example.

Jocelyn just took over an additional team of four managers because their director Linda was promoted. Jocelyn is a newly promoted director herself and becomes completely overwhelmed by the addition of four new managers to her team. With the additional managers, she now has eight managers. All of the managers are based anywhere from twenty to one hundred miles apart so she is having a difficult time spending what she calls "quality time" with any one of them. She believes she is spread too thin.

The four new managers are used to more attention from their previous boss, Linda. They feel neglected and unsupported by Jocelyn. One of the new managers approaches Jocelyn and says that everyone is frustrated with her leadership and they are very unhappy. Jocelyn knows that change makes people uncomfortable and she feels guilty that she isn't doing a better job.

Despite the fact that three of the four managers didn't hit their goals last month, Jocelyn decides not to pursue disciplinary action because the managers' poor performance is probably her fault.

Take a moment and list the facts of this scenario:

_____

_____

_____

_____

_____

_____

_____

What did you come up with? Not sure of all of them? Here they are.

- **Jocelyn has four new managers on her team.**
- **Linda got promoted.**
- **The managers work 20-100 miles apart.**
- **One manager spoke to Jocelyn and referenced other managers.**
- **Three of the four managers did not hit their goals.**
- **Jocelyn does not conduct disciplinary action.**

The rest of this story is all thoughts. Jocelyn is making her situation *mean* something. Her managers are also making the situation mean something. And look at the ultimate outcome. Managers who aren't performing in their roles, aren't held accountable. In fact, their poor performance is ignored by Jocelyn because of her thoughts regarding the situation. Does that make for a strong coach? One manager tells Jocelyn that "everyone" is frustrated and she accepts that as truth. Does that make an effective leader? No. But sadly this is not a unique scenario. This situation is altogether too common in the world of managing. How effective can Jocelyn be as a coach if she honestly believes her managers' lack of performance is her fault? She absolutely believed that 'change makes people uncomfortable.' Who's uncomfortable? She is. So, she believes the thought. Because she believes so passionately, she sought out evidence to prove her thought true. Remember, that thoughts want to find evidence to prove themselves true. It's inherent in the *101 Model*. Thoughts drive feelings, which lead to actions, which lead to results. Jocelyn's belief in her thoughts only supports the poor performing managers on her team to continue to find excuses for their own failures.

Here's how it applies to the Self-Coaching Model.

Circumstance: Linda gets promoted and Jocelyn takes over with eight managers.

Thought: Change makes people uncomfortable.

Feeling: Guilt

Actions: Jocelyn doesn't hold team accountable and is apologetic to team for the changes.

Results: Poor performing team and further evidence that change makes people uncomfortable. *(It's "change's" fault that her managers aren't performing, not the fact that she isn't having any accountability conversations with them.)*

What specific issues are you facing in your work right now? How well can you isolate the facts from thoughts? Initially, most of us aren't very good at it. But with practice you'll find you can ferret out the facts quickly. Doing so is the first step to improving your coaching skill, using the *101 Model*.

Earlier you wrote about your current coaching challenges. Take a moment to review what you wrote. Can you isolate the facts from that story?

Write them here.

_____

_____

_____

_____

_____

_____

_____

_____

_____

_____

_____

_____

_____

_____

_____

_____

(continued)

Now pull out the thoughts.

These would be sentences that you create in your mind that are not based in fact. No matter how hard you try, they cannot be proven true. Opinions are not truths, even if everyone agrees with you.

_____

_____

_____

_____

_____

_____

_____

_____

_____

_____

_____

What you have left is your 'story' or collection of thoughts about the situation. Now you can see how you make facts mean something with your thoughts.

Hopefully, you have a better understanding of how to find the facts or circumstances. You give meaning to circumstances with your thoughts.

Let's explore why those thoughts become so powerful in how you coach your team.

> ### *Here's another example.*
>
>   *"Did you see that John came to work late again today?"* Susan sighed.
>   *"I know," said Joyce. "He totally doesn't care about his job or respect your expectations."*
>   *"You're telling me! He's so disrespectful! He makes me feel so frustrated!" Susan exclaimed. "I'm going to talk with him about it right now!"*

No! Wait! Don't! While I know we've all read in our management books to address issues immediately with our staff, I'm here to tell you that's not always in your best interest, especially if you want to avoid a phone call from your HR Department.

Is Susan in the right place emotionally or mentally to have a constructive conversation with John? Absolutely not! If she went to speak to him right now, it's likely she would address him with exasperation or anger. She may accuse him of being disrespectful of her and the company and create more issues with John. I mean, why the heck would he want to get to work early if his boss is a total jerk, right? Are you with me here?

So let's talk about what happened. John was late. That's it. Susan and Joyce made John's tardiness mean disrespect and lack of interest in his job. When Susan believes that John is disrespectful and disinterested, she feels frustrated. Most of us believe that *John* makes *Susan* feel frustrated. We believe that when someone does something (John being late) we feel something (frustrated). This approach would tell us that circumstances cause feelings, but that is not possible. Circumstances don't cause feelings, thoughts do.

> **Circumstance:** John is late.
>
> **Thought:** John is disrespectful.
>
> **Feelings:** Frustration

It is what you *think* about a circumstance that creates a feeling. Feelings do not occur spontaneously based on a circumstance, I promise. Otherwise, we would all have the same feelings based on the same circumstance. Think of it this way. Two of you go to see a movie. By the end of the movie, you are riveted. You think you may have just seen an Oscar performance. Your friend, on the other hand, started texting half way through because she was so bored. What happened? Did the movie make you riveted and your friend bored? No, a movie can't do that. But what you two were thinking about the movie was very different. The movie doesn't create feelings, your *thoughts* about the movie do.

So what? What's so cool about knowing that you're thoughts create feelings is that you get to pick what you think! Really! What I find so fascinating is that most of us know that we can choose our thoughts and most of us know that thoughts are powerful. I could spend the rest of this book filling it up with quotes from Gandhi, Socrates, and many more on the power of our thoughts. You may even have a few on your desk, on your fridge, or in your planner. Despite the fact that we know this stuff, we don't practice it very well. If we did, we'd have fewer lawsuits, fewer failed marriages, even fewer wars. As Byron Katie says, "All divorce and war begins in the mind."

Think about the relevance this has to you as a manager coach. How many employees have you fired in your mind before you ever gave them the opportunity to succeed? How quickly do you stop coaching when you've decided (thought) that they aren't worth your investment? Now, how brilliant could you be as a coach if you started to identify those thoughts that currently result in poor response, unproductive coaching, and ultimately ineffective leadership? Trust me, you'd be a rock star to your team, and you'd sleep better at night!

Referring back to the example of Susan and John. We know the following:

> **Circumstance:** John is late.
>
> **Thought:** John is disrespectful.
>
> **Feelings:** Frustration

How do you think Susan might act toward John if she is feeling frustrated? She may yell, be abrupt, ignore him, be short, not listen. Any one of these actions could apply.

Let's assume that Susan is abrupt and short with John. What sort of result might she get from her conversation with him?

> **Circumstance:** John is late.
>
> **Thought:** John is disrespectful.
>
> **Feelings:** Frustration
>
> **Action:** Abrupt; short
>
> **Results:** ?

Well, if all thoughts want to be proven true, then she'll get a result that supports her original thought, that John is disrespectful. He might cross his arms, he may stare at her blankly, and he may shrug his shoulders and apologize. How would you act toward someone that was short and abrupt with you? Basically, it doesn't matter what John does, the result will substantiate the thought to Susan. She will also show up as an ineffective coach to John. All because of a thought.

I once worked with a manager who would literally not speak to an employee until after lunch if they were late in the morning. The manager's thoughts and feelings had a definite impact on how she acted as a coach.

Circumstance ⟹ *Thought* ⟹ *Feeling* ⟹ *Action* ⟹ *Results*

There's one more piece to this that's rather interesting to point out. Susan, feeling frustrated with John because she believes *he* is disrespectful, is abrupt and short with him. What do you think about people who are abrupt and short? Any chance you might think *they* are rude or possibly disrespectful? It's not a coincidence that the very thought that Susan has about John (he's disrespectful) drives her to actions that may perpetuate a similar thought about her. Quite fascinating, don't you think?

So what do we know so far? We know that circumstances (facts) happen all the time. Employees do things we can't control. Companies do things we can't control. Those circumstances stand independent of feelings. Our thoughts about the circumstances affect our feelings. When something happens in our life, we make that *mean* something with our thoughts. Our thoughts muster up feelings. It's our feeling state that drives action. When you feeeel happy you might smile. When you feeeel sad you might cry. Based on the actions you take you create a result or outcome. Results that you get from believing a particular thought will always support the original thought.

On page 29, I asked you to reflect on what the thoughts are that you believe about your employees. Just like we saw with Susan, her thought about John led to her feeling frustrated. Now what I want you to do is think about the feelings that come up when you believe the thoughts you wrote down about your employees. Feelings are emotions, like happy, sad, mad, glad, etc. Often times though, people mistake feelings for more thoughts. For example, let's say you have a thought that Jack is rude. I ask you how that thought makes you feel and you respond, "I feel like I wish he wouldn't be that way." That is NOT a feeling, that is another thought. Or maybe you say, "I feel like he should just not work here anymore." Once again, another thought. We all do this. We all express feelings as thoughts. Learning to notice that is powerful. Learning to notice your actual feelings is even more powerful. If our actions stem from how we feel, then we absolutely have to understand what feelings we are experiencing in order to notice ourselves. So, if I ask you how you feel when you believe the thought that Jack is rude, you might say annoyed or angry. You may even say disappointed—all good feeling words, not new, additional thoughts about Jack.

Take a minute to write down the thoughts you have about your employees (from page 29).

Indicate one feeling word with each thought. Remember, a feeling is not another sentence—it is a word.

Thought _____

Feeling _____

Thought _____

Feeling _____

Thought _____

Feeling _____

Thought _____

Feeling _____

(continued)

Thought _____

Feeling _____

So far we've walked through the **Circumstance, Thought** and **Feeling** components of the model.

> **Circumstance:**
>
> **Thought:**
>
> **Feeling:**
>
> **Actions:**
>
> **Results:**

The next step is to realize that your thoughts also determine the actions or behaviors you take. All thoughts want to be proven true, so the feelings that come from the thought will drive actions that lead to results that will prove the thought.

If I believe I'm inadequate, I might feel shameful. If I feel shameful, I may act reclusive. If I act reclusive, I'll continue to get results that prove I'm inadequate because I will have shut myself off from the world to gain new experiences.

> **Thought:**   **I'm inadequate.**
>
> **Feeling:**   **Shameful**
>
> **Actions:**   **Reclusive**
>
> **Results:**   **No new experiences or learning**

Here's another common one with managers.

Thought:	**I need to be liked.**
Feeling:	**Desperate**
Actions:	**Overly accommodating**
Results:	**No accountability on the team**

Situations and people do not make us 'act' a certain way. Our thoughts and feelings drive our actions. As a manager-coach, you have ownership in the performance of your team. If you have performance challenges with people on your team, it's best to start with *your* thinking about *them*. How are you contributing the lack of results? What can you believe differently about the same situation that will lead to you taking new actions?

If you want to change your results, you must change your thoughts. When we focus on solely changing behavior or actions, we are destined for short-term wins, with no long-term success. Most of us are taught as managers that we create results by focusing on activities or actions of the players. So, we write goals around increasing volume in calls, client visits, closed deals, etc. We focus on the activity, hoping to improve results. The truth is, in many cases, you may get short-term improvement. But if the reason 'why' the employee is not meeting his or her expectations in their actions is not addressed, by evaluating their thinking, the old behavior will return. Because thoughts want to prove themselves true.

If I believe I'm inadequate, which is part of why I don't reach out to clients, then no amount of activity goals will help me improve. I'll find a way to prove the thought that I'm inadequate.

That thought will undermine any work you do with me as a coach, because the thought will work hard to prove itself true. As a manager-coach, it's critical that you understand that starting and ending with action, will not give you the lasting results you are looking for. If the goal is to help employees improve and develop, it's imperative that you look at the *thinking* they have that is contributing to their performance challenges. Not on the outcomes alone.

It is our feelings that drive our actions. If I'm feeling angry, I might yell. If I'm feeling sad, I might cry. If I'm feeling happy, I might be more engaged in my work. Feelings drive our actions. It's important to notice how the feelings that you experience determine the actions you take, which lead to your results. If you are feeling angry and you yell at someone at work, what might be the result? Not good, probably. If you are feeling sad and you cry at work, again, not a great result probably. If you are feeling happy and you are more engaged at work, this will likely lead to a positive result.

Reflect on the last exercise. Using the thoughts you believe and subsequent feelings you have, write down the actions you might take based on the feelings you wrote down. What results might you get, based on your actions?

Thought _____

Feeling _____

Action _____

Thought _____

Feeling _____

Action _____

Thought _____

Feeling _____

Action _____

(continued)

Thought _____

Feeling _____

Action _____

Thought _____

Feeling _____

Action _____

Remember that the original thought always will prove itself true by creating a result to support it.

Circumstance:	**John is my employee.**
Thought:	**John is rude**
Feelings:	**Annoyed**
Action:	**I ignore John as much as I can.**
Results:	**I'm rude to John. I don't interact with him to get to know him any better. *(John might think I'm rude)***

What does this all have to do with you as a manager-coach anyway? Well, it has everything to do with you and your overall ability to create and keep a successful team. Great leaders and coaches know that their success has nothing to do with them and everything to do with each individual on the team. Success is in the willingness to be aware of yourself first so that you don't inadvertently get in someone else's way. Effective coaching stems from "understanding someone else's intent" (James Flaherty), and helping them to see how their behavior aligns with their intention. If you, as coach, are so distracted by your own thoughts about employee behavior, how can you help them improve? How can you help them recognize their behavior if all you are doing is speaking to them about your thoughts?

Let's examine this further using the Susan and John situation. Incidentally, I am fascinated by how many managers get totally unglued by employee tardiness. I'm convinced we could feed a small country based on the number of work hours lost while managers conjure up ways to deal with employees who are late. Really fascinating.

Susan is frustrated with John because he is disrespecting her by being late. She is then abrupt with him. The next question we need to explore is "how does Susan's belief that John is disrespectful affect her coaching with John?"

Susan believes John is disrespectful. She feels frustrated and acts abruptly toward John. The result is further distance between them. This impacts Susan's coaching because she isn't focusing on the challenges that John is having. She is not supporting him to find a solution. Rather than gaining understanding and asking John to come up with a plan to resolve the issue, she is telling him what to do. Her coaching is ineffective because there is no plan to improve John's behavior (coming late to work). John is not held accountable to address the issue.

So when Susan believes John is disrespectful, how does that affect the way she coaches him? It might follow something like this.

> *"John, you were late again today and you're behavior is totally disrespectful of me and the company. You are getting a bad reputation around here and people are starting to believe that you are disengaged in your role. I'd suggest if you want your team and I to rely on you as a valuable member, you set your clock back 15 minutes early so that this does not happen again."*

Sound like a reasonably familiar, one-sided 'managereese' kind of conversation? You may not have ever spoken to an employee like this, but someone may have addressed you this way. Right?

This is not coaching behavior from Susan. This is 'telling.' Coaching would be to understand John's intent and then identify a plan to ensure his behavior changes. Susan can certainly tell John that being late in unacceptable, but just telling him won't make his behavior change. The lasting impact occurs by helping John see why he is choosing the behavior and helping him find remedies for change.

So let's think about one of the employees you wrote about in the first exercise. How does what you believe about your employee affect your coaching?

How does your belief about _____
                                  (insert belief about an employee)

_____ **affect the way you coach?**
(insert employee's name)

_____

_____

_____

_____

_____

_____

_____

_____

This is a critical question that can give you really great, insightful information about yourself and the dynamic you create with your team members.

To illustrate this point, I'd like to use another example.

Down the hall, Lucy is also late to work. Her boss Don is all in a lather about her tardiness.

Circumstance:	**Lucy is late.**
Thought:	**She makes me look bad.**
Feelings:	**Angry and embarrassed**
Action:	**Stern; chastising**
Results:	**Manager makes himself look bad to his employees *(matches up with original thought).***

Don sits down with Lucy to discuss the issue. Unlike Susan, who talks about disrespect and lack of job interest, Don tells Lucy that when she is late it is an embarrassment to the team and to him. He explains that she has a responsibility to uphold the reputation of the team (and while he may not say so, he also means himself as the leader).

How does Don's thought that Lucy makes him look bad as a leader affect his coaching? It affects it tremendously. He is coaching Lucy to change her behavior so he will feel better. Since he believes the thought that her tardiness makes him look bad, then he needs her to change so he doesn't feeeeel angry and embarrassed. So he coaches her from his point of view. Think about it, he may as well say "Um, could you please change so that I feel better? That'd be great, thanks!" It's really silly when you see it, but we all do it, all the time. Other people don't need to change for us to feel better. We need to change our thoughts, to change how we feel. Unfortunately, many managers believe that their feelings come from what their employees do and then they manage and coach their staff from that perspective.

I've given you two examples of two employees who have the same performance challenge; being late to work. Because they work for two different managers who make being late mean two very different things, Lucy and John receive very different types of feedback. What is consistent about the feedback is that it is based on their managers' thought about the circumstances. The feedback is all about the managers and not about the employees. The managers believe the thoughts they have about their team members. They believe their team members make them feel a certain way. The subsequent feedback they offer is designed to alleviate their own stress and painful feelings. The coaching has nothing to do with improving the performance of Lucy or John and everything to do with making the managers feel better.

Because the managers, in both examples, believed their negative thoughts about their employees, they forgot one critical component to coach their employees. Can you guess what that might be? What is the one thing we do not know about each employee?

WHY WERE THEY LATE??? This is a point where you have to be honest with yourself as a manager-coach. How many times do you have a "coaching" conversation with an employee without ever exploring their intent? How often to you assume the reasons behind their behavior (your thoughts) and coach with the intent of making yourself feel better? There's no judgment here, we all do it. But I will assert that coaches who can see themselves first in a coaching moment with an employee are much more successful. You can be so much more present for a team member when you aren't trying to change them so you can feel better.

Here's an example of what a conversation might look like with John, if the manager identified his or her own thoughts prior to the coaching conversation.

Manager: John, you were late again today. Can you tell me why?

John: I'm having trouble balancing my wife's new schedule and the new baby's daycare hours.

Manager: I can understand the transition is challenging your previous schedule. As you know, everyone is required to be on time for their shift. What ideas do you have to resolve this issue?

John: I'm not sure; what ideas do you have?

Manager: Well, I'm sure I could brainstorm with you, John, but ultimately you have to be willing to get to work on time. Is that something you are committed to?

John: Absolutely!

Manager: Great, then why don't you work on a plan to ensure you won't be late anymore and we can meet later today to discuss. I'll come up with some ideas for our meeting too. Sound good?

John: Yes.

A few things to note about this conversation:

1. The focus is on why John was late, not on why the manager thinks it's bad that he is late.
2. The manager restated the expectation that all employees, including John be to work on time.
3. The manager reestablished commitment from John to change his behavior.

4. John was asked to come up with a plan and the manager would contribute, not the other way around. Too often, employees ask managers for suggestions. When the suggestions don't work out, it becomes the fault of the manager, not the employee. Accountability is displaced onto the manager, rather than the employee. John is the one who is late; John should create and own his plan.

In this scenario the thoughts of the manager are not interfering with the coaching conversation conducted with John. It's what I like to call "clean." Not charged, not biased, etc. That is ultimately the best space to coach and manage from—when you are focused on the performance, skill, and development of the employee, not making yourself feel better. The trick is to notice when it's happening.

Ok Kris, I can get that circumstances don't create feelings. I get that what I make my circumstances mean creates a thought, which leads to a feeling. I understand that my feelings drive how I act toward my employees and I can even see how those actions perpetuate the negative results. But how do I know it's happening? How do I catch myself so I can be present with my team and not try to fix them so I feel better?

NOTICE YOURSELF FIRST!

The first thing you have to do as a coach is to notice yourself. I'm actually going to ask you to think about yourself in a way that you're not use to. I'm going to ask you to think about how you are feeling and responding to a situation. Instead of thinking about what someone else did to make you feel a certain way, we're going to focus solely on your experience. It won't be about George, Tom, or Sue; it will be only about you.

I can tell when something isn't right, can't you? I think I can even express the feeling states I'm experiencing. I can say I'm sad, happy, fearful, anxious, etc. We tend to express ourselves using feeling words like "that meeting really stressed me out." The trick in using feeling expressions is to attribute the thinking that was going on to drive the feeling. Remember our feelings stem from thoughts that we have about a situation, person, or experience. As we encounter the person or experience, rather than express ourselves in thought, we express ourselves in feeling.

Using the stressful meeting example, most people might say that meeting was really stressful, when what they are 'thinking' could be any number of things:

- *I should be more prepared.*
- *John is always so demanding in the weekly meeting and people shouldn't be demanding.*
- *I never feel like I have the right information for this meeting and I should know everything.*
- *Lisa is such an opportunist. Every time we have this meeting she just tries to position herself in front of the boss. She makes me look bad.*

Expressing our thoughts as feelings is very common. It's common for a few reasons. Generally thoughts that are deeply held are *beliefs*. When our beliefs are challenged, we feeeeeeel a physical response. In fact, your body will usually tell you something is going on before your mind will.

Before I make a presentation I usually have butterflies in my stomach. I'm much more aware of what is happening in my body than what I'm thinking. Although, the physical sensations I'm having are a response to the thoughts I have about making a presentation. If you reflect for a moment, I'm sure you can think of how your body responds to particular situations or people. Those responses happen as a result of what you are *thinking*

I remember sitting with a manager some time ago who had to fire one of her employees. She was a physical mess. She was nervous, stomach hurt and feeling very anxious. Her physical response stemmed from the mess of thoughts she was believing about what *was going* to happen. The employee would get angry, the employee would be dangerous, she (the manager) wouldn't be able to handle him. All these thoughts generated physical responses. She was much more aware of her body and how she was physically feeling, rather than what she was thinking. On the other hand, I had no skin in the game. I wasn't nervous or anxious. I was calm and composed. What was the difference? Our thoughts. I was there to support my manager. She believed she was there to fire an angry, dangerous employee. Because we both made the circumstance mean something different, we both had a very different physical response to the same situation. I'm sure you can find many more examples.

Ever felt a feeling when your boss walks in the room? How about when you have to make a big presentation? How about when you have to fire someone? All of those feeeeelings are evidence about what you are *thinking.* It's important to note that we all do it. All of us respond to our thoughts emotionally and physically. As you work your way through this book it will be really important for you to begin to notice how you are feeeeeling in any situation. That feeling knowledge is critical to self-diagnosis and awareness. Your ability to be self-aware is the cornerstone to your coaching and leading success. I don't think you can pick up a leadership book that has been written in the last 10 years that doesn't expound upon the need for good leaders to have keen self-awareness. Understanding who you are and how you respond to situations is paramount information for coaches and leaders.

Let's take a moment and play with your level of self-awareness.

Write down some feeeeeling words next to the following.
Go with your first reaction.

When I'm with my boss, I feel

_____

List your employees and the feeling word that you attribute to each.

_____

_____

_____

_____

_____

_____

_____

_____

_____

_____

When I don't meet a goal, I feel

_____

When I walked in the door at work today, I felt

_____

When I walked in the door at home today, I felt

_____

(continued)

What's the one thing you enjoy most about being a manager?

_____

When you do this, how do you feel?

_____

What's the one thing you enjoy least about being a manager?

_____

When you do this how do you feel?

_____

How did that feel? (Just kidding). Okay, so the goal of that brief exercise is to help you connect to your feeling states in a couple of situations. For some folks this is really easy to do; for others it's tough. Some people actively experience their feelings daily; others work hard to ignore them. It doesn't make anyone better or worse. It's just information for you to have about how you are expressing and experiencing your world.

As a coach, understanding both the thoughts and the feelings you have creates clarity of perspective you need to be an authentic and powerful coach. It doesn't mean you walk around all day telling people about your feelings. It doesn't mean you become emotional at work. None of that. What it does mean is that the feelings are happening. Your ability to notice them strengthens your compass, strengthens your insight, and reinforces your ability to have consistent and clear coaching conversations. For example if I'm feeling nervous or anxious in my stomach, that's a good queue for me to check my thinking. What thoughts am I having that are generating this physical response? If I'm feeling angry. My heart is racing and I'm flush. What thoughts am I believing that are generating the physical response I'm having?

Here's a quick exercise to 'notice' how you experience emotions, physically:

- **The last time I felt *happy*, I felt** _____

  in my body.

- **The last time I was *angry*, I felt** _____

  in my body.

- **The last time I was *scared*, I felt** _____

  in my body.

In order to start the practice of hearing your own thoughts, before you decide to believe them, you have to know when they are happening. Your body will tell you that you are thinking something that is causing a negative feeling, sometimes before your mind does. Before you act with an employee, notice what is happening for you physically. Your body will tell you. When I get a tingling sensation in my jaw, that's my cue to question what I'm thinking. What am I choosing to believe?

Listening to and feeling what happens in our bodies is a warning mechanism of *junk thinking*. It is how managers and coaches learn to *respond* rather than *react*. When your body tells you something isn't right, explore what is happening with you before you blame someone else for your emotions and subsequent actions.

Your awareness of your thoughts is paramount to effective coaching. Once you've identified a painful or stressful thought, it's time to question your thinking. You'll find that you believe a thought not a fact. It's simply a story or sentence you've conjured up to define a circumstance in your mind.

Now let's explore the thoughts you have around the questions in the previous exercise.

For each statement write one thought that comes up (not a feeling).

When I'm with my boss I think

_____

List your employees and the write one thought that you think about each.

_____

_____

_____

_____

_____

When I succeed in my work I believe

_____

When I don't meet a goal I believe

_____

When I walked in the door at work today I thought

_____

(continued)

When I walked in the door at home today I thought

_____

What's the one thing you enjoy most about being a manager?

_____

What's the one thing you enjoy least about being a manager?

_____

Since we're applying this learning to you as a manager, take a day at work and do the following exercise. Do it for the entire day. See what you find out.

Write down all of the people you interact with and the experiences you had during the course of the day. Label each person and or experience with a feeling word (happy, sad, worried, nauseous, etc.).

_____

_____

_____

_____

_____

_____

_____

(continued)

_____

_____

_____

_____

_____

_____

Now, take each person/experience and the feeling state and see if you can come up with a thought you had while dealing with that person or while you were in the experience. (He talks too much, this meeting is boring, etc.)

_____

_____

_____

_____

_____

_____

_____

_____

_____

(continued)

_____

_____

_____

_____

_____

_____

   The purpose of this exercise is to start to notice how you feel because of what you think in situations at work. As we continue to discuss, it is critical for you as coach to realize that your thoughts do not 'happen' to you from an external source. They are created by you. You think a thought and you feel the response of that thought emotionally and physically. That's that. Other people, situations, experiences, etc. do not create your feelings; your thoughts create your feelings. You choose your thoughts. To be an effective coach, you must notice what is happening to you. I started this section by saying you would focus on yourself. I was referring to noticing yourself, what you're thinking, and the feelings that ensue. The thoughts you have determine how you impact your team. Your self-awareness helps you to remain objective and clear in your approach and ultimately in your coaching.

Here's a quick example of how thinking and feelings impact behavior in a work environment and how you can notice yourself in the moment.

   Ann is in a meeting with her boss and her peers. They are brainstorming to find a solution for a problem that has just been identified. Given Ann's experience, she believes she has tremendous value to offer and begins to share her ideas.

(continued)

After her third idea, her boss thanks her and asks her to hold off on any other ideas until the rest of the team has offered some suggestions as well. Ann immediately glares at her boss, crosses her arms, and starts doodling on her notepad. She disengages from the discussion and that's not good for anyone. Her face feels hot and she begins to feel tight in her stomach.

Ann can tell she's feeling something, but what? Why? What is she thinking?
Here's what Ann can do, right there on her notepad. She can use the Self-Coaching Model.

What am I thinking that has created this physical response?

Here's how this looks in the Self-Coaching Model:

Circumstance:	**Boss says hold off on any other ideas.**
Thought:	**He doesn't like my ideas.**
Feelings:	**Embarrassed**
Action:	**Disengaged**
Results:	**No more ideas shared.**

Ann starts to act totally different, simply because of her interpretation of her boss' comments. She made his words 'mean' something to her in her own thoughts, which had a direct impact on her feelings and behavior in the meeting. She certainly could have chosen a totally different thought, right? She could have thought, "I'm smarter and more engaged than my coworkers." But she didn't. She chose to believe that her boss doesn't like her ideas. That's not effective and isn't going to get her to demonstrate peak performance in this (or possibly other) team meetings.

So, the answer to knowing if you have ineffective thoughts is as easy as starting to pay attention to yourself and how you are experiencing situations around you. Listen to your body; listen to your mind. Hear the thoughts you are having and write them down.

Observation of your thinking is critical. Then applying the *101 Model* to the thought allows you to *deconstruct* it and see the potential outcome of believing the thought. The pen is your friend when you believe a stressful thought. When you are lit up about a person or situation, sit down and write about it. It doesn't have to take long, just long enough to find the thought that's conjuring up a mess in your body and your mind.

SO I HAVE IDENTIFIED INEFFECTIVE THOUGHTS, NOW WHAT?

It's one thing to realize you are having negative thoughts about your team; it's another to figure out what to do about it. The next step in the process is to begin to find alternative thoughts, or replacement thoughts that are believable. Since we know that we can manage our minds, then we can be an active participant in the thoughts we choose to believe. Thoughts determine how we feel, which leads to our actions and results. To change our behavior and our outcomes, we must change our thoughts. They must be believable for this to work. You can't just make stuff up. And we're not talking about the 'power of positive thinking,' mantras, etc.

Making up a thought that isn't real to you isn't effective, and it won't last. Sometimes an alternate thought may not seem to be more positive, but if it makes you feeeel better, and in turn you act differently, then it's a good thought. That's why spending time on thinking through other things you can believe about a person or situation is a powerful exercise. The thought has to be one that you can believe—not just something that sounds good.

When I say rework the thought, here's what I mean.

Let's take Susan and John's example again.

We left off here.

Circumstance: **John is late.**

Thought: **John is disrespectful.**

Feeling: **Frustrated**

Actions: **Abrupt; short**

Results: **Susan is rude to John and he probably will keep being late.** *(and oh-by-the-way, Susan isn't holding John accountable to why he's being late.)*

Susan has seen the light and doesn't want to be abrupt and short with John anymore. But she isn't sure how to change that behavior. We need to help Susan rework her thinking and find an alternative thought that will help her respond differently to John. Remember, the circumstance of John being late hasn't changed.

There are a few ways to go about identifying a new thought. The first one is to ask yourself what else you can believe about John that is true, that doesn't evoke negative feelings. "Can I believe he's trying? Can I believe he's a good guy? What can I believe?" Sometimes that's hard for managers because they really can't find a new thought that works.

Another way to play around with finding an alternative thought is to ask yourself "okay, how do I want to feel when I'm coaching or working with this employee?" From that question you may be able to find some feeling words that resonate for you and help you find the thought that conjures that feeling.

Let's say that Susan says she wants to feel relaxed around John; she wants to feel calm when he's late. If she wants to feel "relaxed" and "calm," what does she have to believe about John or herself that will drive those feelings the next time he's late? Make sense?

Here's how it looks.

Circumstance:	**John is late.**
Thought:	**John is effective when he's here.**
Feeling:	**Calm, relaxed**
Actions:	**Meet with John, approach him, and ASK him how being late is affecting his work**
Results:	**Conversation is focused on John and his issue, not on Susan and her frustration.**

By changing her thought, Susan is able to approach the conversation with John from a totally different perspective. As a result, her behavior (actions) will be different. It's likely that she will have a completely different conversation and she will be more effective.

What's important about applying the *Self-Coaching Model* is that no matter what John gives as an excuse, it doesn't have to bug Susan. She can listen to his story about why he's late, and then move forward. From a relaxed and calm feeling, she can remind him of the expectation, ask if there's anything she can do to support him in being to work on time, and finally tell him she'll expect him to be to work on time daily. There's no pain in the conversation, John is clear about the expectation, Susan isn't fretting and most importantly an employee is held accountable for his behavior. It's beautiful!

At the end of the day, you as manager-coach are responsible for harnessing and maximizing the resources of your organization. The biggest resources you have are your employees. The only way you will ever maximize those resources is if you communicate effectively, share information, and support employee development. By focusing on their challenges, performance, etc. and not your stories about them, you will be more effective than you are today.

"No snowflake in an avalanche ever feels responsible."
~ George Burns

3

THE COACH AND ACCOUNTABILITY

P oor performance, lack of productivity, and lack luster individual results are issues for all organizations. Every company has employees who are not maximizing their time, efforts, and results. Consequently, organizations are not performing at optimal levels. They are not utilizing their resources in the best way possible. Organizations hire managers to ensure goals are met at every level. In my work coaching leaders, I have found that the primary roadblock to success, at all levels of the organization, is a failure to follow through with accountability.

Leaders avoid conversations that they believe will be difficult, and because they avoid conversations about poor performance, the poor performance continues. If we can help our leaders understand 'why' they avoid those conversations and remove lack of accountability as a stumbling block to results, we can improve the production and success of their companies.

In addition to improving performance, you'll also improve the respect and reputation of the leaders within the organization. If you have ever been a top performer and watched a poor performer continue to squeak by, then you know what I'm referring to. There's nothing more frustrating (from an employee's perspective) to know how hard you are working and to watch as poor performers continue on because their manager doesn't deal properly with the situation.

Employees expect their leaders to be clear and consistent. When managers aren't, they systematically lose buy-in and respect from their staff. That lack of respect can further erode the ability of an organization to be productive and successful. Applying the Self-

Coaching model is one of the surest ways to move the needle within your organization.

Accountability is my favorite topic of discussion with manager-coaches. Your ability to create an environment of accountability is critical to long-term success. There is no doubt that your team wants to know:

a) Where is the goal line?
b) How will you respond if they don't reach it?

Your experience and thoughts about accountability determine these two things. Although you may never say it out loud, you can be sure that your team knows exactly where you stand on the matter. They are watching you and paying close attention to how consistent, fair, and balanced you are in your approach to performance.

First let's define accountability. Dictionary.com says

> **accountable**
>
> — *adi*
>
>> **responsible to someone or for some action; answerable**

You've probably heard of "holding your team or others accountable." I contend that you can't actually 'hold' someone accountable. What would that look like anyway? How do you 'hold' someone accountable? There is only one person you can hold accountable and that's you. You can hold yourself accountable to having a conversation with an employee when they do or don't meet the expectations of the position, a project, or assignment. Good coaches do this all the time. That's to say that having an accountability conversation is not an "event." It is woven into an effective coach-employee relationship.

I want you to think about what I just said. Accountability, the act of addressing a performance gap or performance problem, is an ongoing practice. It isn't a once-in awhile, "please come to my office," moment or event.

Managers who hold infrequent coaching conversations leave room for the dramatic. They tend to lose the point of holding consistent expectations and they freak everyone out. Who wants to work for the guy or gal who makes a production out of poor performance, only when things are going really poorly? Don't we all want to know the first time we mess up, rather than when it's a big deal?

For example, imagine a manager that had a file that was a unique color. He would only use that folder with an employee when he was going to write them up for poor performance. He would call out an employee's name in front of everyone, tap the folder, and tell them to go into his office. Now, seriously, what is the point of that? To freak people out? Scare them?

We all hold beliefs and thoughts about performance and accountability. As a result, most managers avoid accountability conversations and some handle them in a ridiculous fashion. Why? Because they are afraid: afraid of confrontation, afraid of disappointment, afraid they'll hurt someone's feelings, or afraid their employees will cry. Feel free to insert your thoughts here.

Manager's don't like to hear they are afraid. They often get defensive and say they just aren't "good" with conflict. Whatever you want to call it, it is what it is. I'm not sure when accountability at work became correlated with conflict, but it is a pretty consistent reason why managers avoid conversations with their employees.

Why is having a conversation with someone who missed a goal a conflict? And why do managers coach their employees believing they are responsible for their employees' response? Is it actually possible to control how someone else will respond to you? No! The only person you can manage is you. The reality is, if you effectively manage and understand yourself you will be much more capable of delivering a sound, reasonable message that is more likely to be 'heard' by your team.

Let's take a moment to expound upon the concept of being responsible for other peoples' reactions. I realize that we are generally raised not to do hurtful and outright mean things to other people. That's not what I'm talking about. What I am referring to is the common issue (especially for managers) of not wanting to do or say something to someone because of how they may potentially respond.

Managers make assumptions of how others will respond based upon their experience with particular individuals. Sometimes the *thoughts* about how someone will respond are based upon our own experience and how we would respond if someone did or said something similar to us.

Regardless, it is not possible to predict or control how someone responds to us. There is nothing I can do, short of living in someone else's mind, to know absolutely what someone will do. I cannot change who I am to control someone else's actions.

The sooner we all come to terms with the ridiculous notion of being able to manage someone else's responses, the freer we become to authentically coach and manage to the goals and outcomes we are responsible for. So managing your team, based upon what you think your employees may or may not do is not a sound practice. It generally leads you to avoid critical conversations you need to have.

Think about the following scenario.

A director (Eric) has a manager (Alan) on his team who is known throughout the organization as unprofessional, a poor leader, and disrespectful of authority. Alan, the manager, has worked for the company for more than four years has had three managers, and no one has been committed to help him improve his performance or exit gracefully.

(continued)

The director-coach, Eric, finds himself constantly annoyed with his employee. Alan knows this and baits him. In fact, in one of their most recent interactions, Eric raised his voice and dismissed the employee from his office. Not a terribly effective manager-coach behavior.

Here are Eric's comments about Alan.
- **He's always in and out of my office.**
- **He's disrespectful.**
- **His team can't stand him.**
- **He's dishonest.**
- **He doesn't do what I ask.**
- **He is always in control of the conversation.**

When one simple word 'and' is added, here's what Eric makes those comments mean.

- **He's always in and out of my office. *AND*... he should know better, he's intentionally interrupting me.**
- **He's disrespectful. *AND*... I feel inadequate.**
- **His team can't stand him. AND...I feel like I'm letting them down.**
- **He's dishonest. *AND*... people shouldn't lie.**
- **He doesn't do what I ask. *AND*... he should because I'm his boss.**
- **He is always in control of the conversation. *AND*...I get really angry.**

By asking AND after each statement, we get more insight into our director-coach. We find out his thoughts about Alan.

Here's what we know about the <u>thoughts</u> Eric has about Alan.

- He believes his employee is an interruption.
- He feels inadequate around his employee.
- He's letting the whole team down.
- People should do what he says.
- His employee makes him angry.

What's the common theme? Have you got it? Eric is making Alan's behavior mean something about his leadership. Eric's focus is actually on his own thoughts about Alan. How much of what Eric is experiencing has anything to do with his employee? Here's the short answer, zero. Everything Eric is dealing with is his 'stuff'— thoughts and his very elaborate story about this employee. This coach struggles to hold his boundaries. By not managing his own thoughts about Alan, Eric is losing his effectiveness as a manager and a coach. He is also not helping Alan either improve or exit.

Let's look at each one of these thoughts to see how we could help him resolve this issue so he can be a better coach.

To continue the example, let's work through each one.

Circumstance:	**Alan walked into my office (provable fact, outside of Eric's control)**
Thought:	**He shouldn't interrupt me.**
Feeling:	**Annoyed**
Actions:	**Short, rude**
Results:	**Inadequate attention paid to the Alan. Leads employee to continue impromptu visits.**

Here's Eric's reworked thought to achieve a different result.

Circumstance: Alan walked into my office.

Thought: I manage my own time

Feeling: Strong, Confident

Actions: Redirect, ask him to schedule a better time to chat

Results: Dedicated, scheduled time with the employee *(and probably fewer impromptu visits)*

Here's another.

Circumstance: Alan crosses his arms and rolls his eyes.

Thought: He is disrespectful.

Feeling: Inadequate, angry

Actions: Confrontational conversation. Said, "What's your problem?"

Results: Eric is actually the one acting disrespectfully to the employee. *(Notice how the thought that the coach has about his employee "he is disrespectful" is actually driving the same behaviors from Eric–being confrontational– that would lead to the employee thinking the same thing about the coach.)*

Rework the thought.

Circumstance:	Alan rolls crosses arms and rolls eyes.
Thought:	It's good that he's acting exactly as I expect him to.
Feelings:	Calm, content
Action:	Patient
Result:	As coach, you stay calm. No more conflict instigated by the coach.

Example:

Circumstance:	The team has a manager named Alan.
Thought:	I'm letting them down.
Feelings:	Helpless, embarrassed
Action:	Over involved with the staff
Results:	Eric is undermining Alan by being too involved with the staff. He's letting the manager down, by not demonstrating trust, autonomy, etc.

Reworked:

Circumstance:	The team has a manager named Alan.
Thought:	I have strong and capable employees.
Feelings:	Confident
Action:	Trust that work is getting done; when issues arise, resolve them via Alan.
Results:	Direct employees to Alan

The thing that is important to note here is just because you change your thought doesn't mean their poor performance doesn't need to be addressed.   In fact, by clearing your own thinking, you are more capable of having an accountability conversation. If Alan the manager, is not properly managing his team and is creating performance, morale, etc. problems, then those issues must be addressed. But when poor performance is addressed by a manager, it must be done so with *clean* thinking. Otherwise, you will bring in too much of your own stuff and will not effectively communicate, inquire, and understand the issues related to the employee's performance problem.

Here's the last thought between Eric the director and Alan the manager.

Circumstance:	Alan didn't complete an assignment on time.
Thought:	He doesn't have to do what I tell him to do, but he should.
Feelings:	Anger, resentment, disappointed
Action:	Extended 'talk' with Eric regarding why he should have done the project on time. Eric spends all of his time speaking and talking and very little asking and inquiring of Alan.
Results:	There's no real consequence *(other than listening to Eric go on and on)* for not completing the assignment.

Reworked:

Circumstance:	Alan didn't complete an assignment on time.

(continued)

New Thought:	**I follow through on my commitments.**
Feelings:	**Emboldened, powerful**
Action:	**Speak to Alan about desired outcomes for the assignment. Clearly outline expectations for the assignment and consequences for not meeting the deadline.**
Results:	**I hold myself accountable to manage Alan's outcomes.**

Another note here, because this issue has come up frequently with other managers. People are going to miss deadlines. Some employees, however, are much more consistent with missing deadlines than others. If you ask an employee to deliver on a deadline, that's what the expectation is. As long as you have been clear and concise with your instruction, the deadline is firm.

Many managers, however, continue to dance with their non-deadline meeting employees, rather than holding a clear commitment to the expectation. Once Eric has reworked his thought, he is focused now on following through with his commitments. His commitment in this case is to hold Alan accountable for completing the assignment, not to let him off the hook because he didn't finish, and not to tell him why what he did is bad, unacceptable or to preach to him. No, hold yourself accountable for having the clear conversation with him for not following through. There's a consequence for not completing the plan on time, but the expectation is that the plan will still be completed. When this has happened with other leaders, here's a recommendation I often make.

When the employee arrives for their scheduled meeting with an incomplete assignment, tell him/her you will postpone the meeting until later that day, maybe until 3:00 pm. This gives them the time they need to complete the work. If they still don't have it done by 3:00 pm, reschedule the meeting for the next day at 10:00 am to review the work. Remember, it's his/her work, not yours. There's no reason for any conflict/confrontation here. Your job is to hold the expectation, nothing more. As her manager you'll also need to document each time she misses a deadline. Accountability in any environment is to ensure that someone accepts responsibility for his or her actions. Within an organization that usually means formal and informal disciplinary action.

My point here is, you don't have to have poor thoughts that generate unpleasant feelings (in fact you shouldn't if you want to be effective) to hold someone to an expectation. In fact, you are actually more effective when you get your thoughts out of the way and concentrate on the employee.

The important point of this scenario is that the Director did change his thoughts about Alan. He became more confident, more controlled, and was no longer frazzled by his relationship with the manager. Eventually, Alan left the organization.

Coaching is about helping people get from "here" to "there," remember. "There" doesn't always have to be within the organization. Often times the best gifts we give others is the freedom to move on. When you think about it, how happy could Alan have been? He had a poor performing team who didn't respect him, didn't trust him. He also had a leader who wasn't investing in him because he was so caught up in his own thoughts. One can only hope that Alan will learn from this experience and evaluate what he was thinking that led him to failed performance.

Accountability is the crux of organization success. Leaders need to know what their core beliefs are around accountability if they are going to communicate effectively the performance gaps and issues. The first step to gain understanding is to learn what you believe about poor performance and accountability.

We all have a collection of beliefs around these two subjects that make up our story. That story is what we tell ourselves when we are dealing with poor performance, and consequently it becomes how we define each circumstance. Rather than acknowledging and noticing the factual circumstance, we use our beliefs to define what is happening. As a result we feel a certain way that leads us to act a certain way and ultimately glean results that probably don't get us what we want.

Do you have a consistent pattern of poor performance on your team? Similar performance issues, possibly on different teams with different companies, may be the result of a collection of beliefs that are perpetuating a similar outcome. The first step then is to determine what your beliefs and thoughts are related to poor performance and accountability and see how that impacts your leadership and coaching.

The following exercise is designed to help you connect with your thoughts, see how they may be effecting your leadership role, and how willing you are to conduct conversations around accountability. Here is an example of someone else's "story" regarding accountability.

What is your belief about *accountability*?

I shouldn't have to 'hold people accountable.' People should act like grown-ups and be responsible for themselves.

1. **Why do you believe this?**
   Because people should just know that they should work hard and meet expectations.
2. **Why (rephrase thought above) should people just know that they should work hard and meet expectations?**
   Because I do.

(continued)

3. **Why (rephrase thought above) do you meet expectations?**

    Because if I don't, I'll disappoint someone.

4. **Why (rephrase thought above) don't you want to disappoint someone?**

    Because then they'll be upset with me and think poorly of me.

5. **Why (rephrase thought above) is it bad if others are upset with you and think poorly of you?**

    Then I guess I feel inadequate and invaluable.

How does your belief (insert #5 answer here) affect or impact your coaching others on accountability?

I don't talk with people when they aren't performing because I resent the fact that they are making me do it. They should know better (like I do) and therefore, it seems unfair that I have to have the conversation.

What potential roadblocks to holding others accountable may present themselves, based on your story and beliefs?

Because I'm concerned about my own belief that I might be invaluable or inadequate, I'm actually not helping others improve. By not having conversations about performance, I'm perpetuating the results that confirm that I'm inadequate. Because if my team isn't performing, then neither am I.

> ***How can you reframe your belief to have a positive effect on your outcomes?***
>
> | | |
> |---|---|
> | **Circumstance:** | **Team member is not performing.** |
> | **Thought:** | **I can provide guidance to my employee.** |
> | **Feelings:** | **Valued, important, relevant** |
> | **Action:** | **Talk with employee about performance, focus on employee's needs** |
> | **Results:** | **Provide guidance and support. Address performance gaps. It's likely performance will improve.** |

Our stories about what accountability is determines how we show up as coaches. In my experience, whatever you learned in your personal and professional life supports the type of approach you take when conducting conversations around performance gaps and challenges. For example, if you lived in a family where accountability was in the form of yelling if you failed or didn't meet your parents expectations, that experience will likely show up in your leadership and coaching. You may react in a similar fashion, be hot headed and externalize your anger. Or you might not want to show any emotion, since your experience with such overt expressions of disappointment were hurtful, etc.

If accountability for you was silence then you knew you didn't meet expectations when people in your life just ignored it—or you. As a leader, you are likely to use the same strategy. Follow along? Does this make sense? Your patterns come from your beliefs and your thoughts tell you how to feel in a situation where accountability is to be addressed.

This is where you get really honest. What do you do when you have to address a performance challenge at work? Do you explore the issue with the employee? Or just tell them how they need to change? Is it a one sided conversation? Or is the employee involved in the discussion? Many managers override their discomfort by over-talking and controlling the conversation. Not allowing the employee to participate or share their perspective and ideas, gives the manager a perception of control.

When managers ignore failed performance they are actually speaking really loudly. When managers don't address poor performance, they are giving permission for the behaviors and results to continue. Without realizing it, lack of communication perpetuates the very thing that drives the thoughts and subsequent feelings. I find it fascinating. When managers ignore behaviors because of discomfort, they are hoping the behaviors will miraculously change. But the reality of it is that managers are only prolonging their discomfort by not addressing the challenges.

Here's an example from my past.

I had an employee whom I didn't trust. Let's call her Linda. Linda was dishonest (by my assessment, and as a result, our relationship worsened because of my thinking.)

Circumstance:	**Employee did things during work hours that weren't related to her job.**
Thought:	**She is dishonest.**
Feelings:	**Anger, disappointment**
Action:	**Avoided her, disengaged from her, guarded**
Results:	**A dishonest relationship - both she and I were not being honest with each other.**

And who would trust a boss that avoids them, is guarded, and is disengaged with them?

The fact was she *was* doing something that she shouldn't during work hours. But because of the thoughts I had about her (being dishonest), I never had the conversation with her to address the issue. So two things happened. She continued to do things she wasn't supposed to do, and I continued to gather evidence of how dishonest she was. Brilliant!

The employee continued to conduct herself inappropriately, during company time, and I continued to get annoyed. Highly practical method of leading and coaching, wouldn't you say?

So back to your being honest with yourself. How do you react when you have to address a performance gap or issue?

Think of a situation you have been struggling with and fill out this worksheet.

When an employee doesn't meet expectations I think

_____

_____

This thought makes me feel

_____

_____

When I feel this way I act

_____

_____

(continued)

When I act this way, the results I get are

_____

_____

What you are thinking determines how you feel and ultimately act. You as manager-coach are responsible for overall team performance. You've been hired to deliver outcomes for your organization. The way you achieve those results is by harnessing the talent of the people that work for you.

You can't talk it, yell it, and ignore it out of them. You have to understand them to help them, and the first person you have to understand is yourself. I know that in many ways that's a HUGE bummer! Many managers I've worked with really, really believe that poor performance is the fault of their employees. If their employees would just be better, more talented, more committed, more responsible, more, more, more... Guess what, they could be if their manager did *Thought* work and held their employees accountable. Managers would then be the leaders they wanted to be, with the team they wanted to have. Poor team performance is yours to own.

Let's take look a look at some information that is relevant and current in your work. Using the exercise you did at the beginning of this book, what performance issue is occurring on your team, right now?

What is the circumstance? (Remember, must be factual and provable, not just corroborated by others)

_____

_____

(continued)

What thought do you have regarding this circumstance?

_____

_____

What feelings do you have when you believe this thought?

_____

_____

What actions do you take (specifically with this employee) when you feel these feelings?

_____

_____

What results are YOU getting? (Focus on *you* here, not the employee.)

_____

_____

Remember that the thought will always find evidence to prove itself true. What are you doing that is supporting the original thought?

_____

_____

(continued)

Now here's the kicker question.

> **How are you showing up as a coach to this employee? (Be honest! Saying that you don't really act differently is not a truth and you know it!)**
>
> _____
>
> _____
>
> _____
>
> _____

What do you think? Are you an effective coach for your employee? One of the things I often say to managers I work with who are dealing with performance issues, is that you always want to know you gave someone all you could before you move forward with any sort of disciplinary action. Right? They deserve that of you as their manager-coach. When you are clear about your own thinking, you can be completely present for your employee. Then, if out of that coaching experience they are unable or unwilling to change their performance, then that is their choice. Not just their response to your ineffective coaching.

So let's relook at the performance challenge you just wrote about and let's make an attempt to flip it. What I've found to be pretty consistent is that when managers have unwelcome feelings associated with an employee, they have to start there (rather than with their thoughts). Feelings can speak a lot louder and can also be easier to determine. So let's try it this way:

Thinking of the employee you just wrote about, how do you want to FEEEEEEEEL when you are working with them on their performance challenge?

Write those feeling words here.

When I work with _____,

I want to *feeeeeel* _____.

When I *feeeeeeel* _____

with _____,

I will *act* _____

_____.

When I *act* _____

with _____,

the *results* **I will get are** _____

_____

_____.

What can you believe about your employee that will drive the feelings you wrote about? Remember, you have to believe this thought. This is NOT about the power of positive thinking. This is about finding an alternative thought that can generate new feelings, new actions, and new results. This is not a mantra you put on your computer or your fridge. This is something you can believe today.

Thought I can believe about my employee that drives the feeling I want:

_____

_____

Once you identify a new, believable thought, you give your mind somewhere else to go. Instead of believing that your employee is lazy and a jerk, you can believe he is misunderstood. You can believe he needs your help. You can believe you are capable of supporting his goals. You can believe he is a good guy. There's always something else you can believe about someone on your staff that will evoke feelings that ultimately drive better results.

There's a key in all this work, especially related to accountability. It's to notice yourself first before you address your staff member. If you are frustrated, angry, annoyed, hurt, etc., that is your trigger that you believe a thought that is putting you in an ineffective coaching space. As a manager-coach, it is your responsibility to catch yourself before you coach from that place.

Your feelings will tell you if you believe a painful thought. When you notice that, make it about you, not someone else. What I mean by that is that most managers will blame their discomfort, frustration, and pain on their employees. Right? If so and so would just change, come to work on time, work harder, etc., I would feel better. But that's not how it works. _Other people don't need to change for you to feel better_. You need to evaluate what you are thinking to make yourself feel better. You need to change your thoughts.

Then, through those thoughts will come positive feelings and constructive actions. You will be an effective and powerful coach. That's the truth. I've lived, seen it, I know it.

"Let us merely separate ourselves from the crowd,
and we shall be made whole."
~ Seneca

4

TEAM THINK AND THE COACH

W e've spent the majority of discussion about you as a leader and how *your thoughts* determine how you act as a coach to your employees. I want to spend some time now talking about how *team thoughts* or *organization thoughts* impact the overall performance of a group or organization. The best way to kick this off is to start with a real example.

Situation:

The way that XYZ had managed, evaluated, and paid its front line employees had to be changed. As a result, the organization made the decision to remove the current compensation plan and performance management tools. Now, there are many factors involved in this situation. Changing employees' compensation plan can give rise to numerous emotions and thoughts..

Here's what happened in this case. The change occurred at the beginning of the first quarter of the year. Within three months, an organization that has traditionally thrived financially took a steep performance dive.

So what happened? Why the significant performance breakdown?

(continued)

> *Were people not motivated anymore? (Thought) Were they disengaged with the changes? (Thought) Did they no longer trust their leadership? (Thought). There were many individual thoughts going on at the time. But there were a few pervasive 'team thoughts' that were doing the big damage.*
>
> *In coaching many folks during this time, the most common thought was, "I won't be able to hold my people accountable."*

Circumstance: **Compensation has changed.**

Thought: **I won't be able to hold my people accountable.**

Feelings: **Nervous, scared, worried, anxious, angry**

Actions: **Paralyzed, shut down, disengaged**

Real quick for all you leaders out there… what kind of results do you get when your leadership team is acting paralyzed, shut down, and disengaged?

Results: **Significantly lower results than ever before *and* managers not holding staff accountable.**

That original, powerful thought of "I won't be able to hold my people accountable" came true! Because a group of leaders believed that they wouldn't be able to hold people accountable to their results without the plan, they completely checked out. And guess what? Their people knew it! And they stopped working, because they could. Because they had a leadership team walking around BELIEVING they wouldn't be able to do anything any way.

How crazy is that? This is an example of a powerful, limiting group thought.

I hope you are recognizing the power behind the thoughts you create in your mind and the power behind believing other peoples' thoughts. The situation with this organization started with a few folks and spread like wildfire. Because there were teams who were already not performing, they were quickly able to find evidence to prove the thought—they weren't able to hold their people accountable. And it grew and grew and grew until it had a dramatic impact. Fascinating!

What other examples can you think of? How about working for leaders who have a scarcity approach? They believe there will never be enough resources or that the company will run out of business. What kind of group thoughts does that behavior create? What about leaders who play to the street all the time? They drive their business to look good to shareholders rather than employees. What type of environment and culture does that create and sustain? What about teams? Can you think of some team-think that have adversely affected the overall performance of the team?

Recently, I observed an organizational meeting. It was a sales meeting with about 30 managers, a few VP's and the CEO. The company is relatively small, not a huge annual revenue budget. Most years they earned about $70 million. During the CEO's presentation, he shared with the team how the new fiscal year was bringing significant change. That the goals were going up. In fact, they were now going to expected to close the next fiscal year with $100 million in revenue. But, there wasn't going to be any on-the-ground growth. All increases in revenue were expected to come from individual contributions, by each employee, at each satellite location.

As I watched his presentation, I felt unnerved. He was directing the room to understand his expectations. He had really pretty PowerPoint slides, with arrows and charts, etc. But something wasn't right. I leaned over to my colleague who worked in the organization and said to him, "He doesn't believe you guys can achieve the goals he's talking about, does he?" He looked at me and shook his head.

Here's how I knew the boss didn't believe it. These are some of the statements he made:

"I know it's gonna be tough guys, but we gotta do this, this year, I mean it."

"You're going to have to expect more from your people"

If you had been in the room, you would have heard his voice too. There was not much strength in it. He was almost apologetic. He was definitely feeeeeeeling something, that was making him act, frankly, weak. I can't be sure what his actual thoughts were, because I didn't ask him and he didn't volunteer. But here's an example of actions he took. *Note: I guessed his thought based on my observation of his presentation.*

---

*C- **Tenured manager not meeting revenue goals***

*T- (guess) **The goals I've outlined for my people aren't realistic.***

*F- **Inadequate, weak***

*A- **Doesn't let the regional leader fire a tenured manager for not performing.***

*R- **Manager keeps up non-performance. Other managers know that the goals aren't really important and they don't achieve them either.***

Unfortunately, this is a perfect example of how the thoughts of the CEO can impact the results of an entire organization. Your thoughts govern your decisions. If you are the CEO and you don't believe in your own plan, you have a problem. It won't take long for your subordinates to realize they can wiggle around in all the space you've left them. Or they will struggle with trying to maneuver through a confusing performance landscape when the lines aren't clear. The performance of the company relies on clear thinking of its leadership.

When I created my first coaching team I was tremendously excited. This was something that had never been done before in my organization, and it was a tremendous opportunity to build and create as I needed to.

One of the things that I believed to be true about this entire experience was that it was my credibility that was on the line. I believed that I got the role because of the respect and credibility I'd garnered over my years with the company. Therefore, I was sure not going to let anything happen to adversely affect the perceived credibility I thought I had. (Do you see where this is going?? Have you already identified some of my thoughts and how they may have affected my team?)

One of the things I used to say to my teammates frequently is "Did you add value today?" We didn't have any gauge to determine how we were performing so that seemed like a reasonable, daily assessment to ensure we were doing our best. As it turns out it was a horrible question for me to be asking of my team. There are several reasons why it was ineffective.

- **Who decides if something is valuable? (thoughts)**
- **Did you provide value today? That can be answered with a "no," right?**
- **It drove the team to worry about not adding value.**

Each person on my team interpreted that question "did I add value today?" differently. As a result, not only did I create the group thought listed below, but they each had their own thoughts.

Check this out.

Here's the example of the group thought.

Circumstance:	**New team**
Thought:	**We must add value or I will look bad.**
Feelings:	**Pressured, stressed**
Actions:	**Rapid pace of work, working too many hours, working to please others**

The thought "we must add value" took on a different meaning for each member of the team. Sometimes I find it helpful to write down, what I call spider thoughts, to the original thought. So there's sort of an anchor thought and then there are also other thoughts that spring off of that one. In this case, the leader's thought created several different thoughts for each of the team members.

Here's what a spider thought map might look like.

So each person on my team was making "we must add value today" mean something else to them. But the overall effect was the same. That one thought of mine was in many ways debilitating the team's performance. While you couldn't see it on the 'outside,' we were rapidly free falling, each one of us. We had to reevaluate that thought and recognize it was no longer vibrant. It was through our work with Brooke Castillo that we were able to come up with a new *Primary Question* that emboldened us as team.

WHAT IS A PRIMARY QUESTION?

A Primary Question is a question that you repetitively ask yourself all the time. All of us do this, without much attention. What we learned from Brooke is that we first have to notice what the question is, conduct a self-coaching model on it, (to see what it is doing to you to be asking yourself that question), and then find another question. What's really important with the question is that it can't be able to be answered 'no.' Asking did you?, did I?, am I?, are you? types of questions won't work. The question needs to be answered with information and further evidence, not a yes or a no.

In the case of my team, we decided we didn't like "Did I bring value today?" Instead we chose the question "How can we create kick-ass leaders?" This question worked for us. We even started giving each other theme gifts around the kick-ass reference. It stuck and it empowered and emboldened all of us to show up very differently in our work. It was at that point that our team started to flourish with our external customers and within the group. Once everyone stopped believing all their stressful thoughts about their value and starting looking for evidence of how they created a kick-ass leader that day. It was amazing!

The following example shows some key points:

1. The thoughts of the leader show up in the team.

2. The thoughts of the leader create group thoughts and individual thoughts that support or challenge the performance of the team.

3. Thoughts can have a bunch of spider thoughts that all need to be looked at.

4. We all ask ourselves a primary question. We need to notice it, work on it and then reframe it.

Now it's your turn. I want you to think for a moment about a couple of things. What thoughts are pervasive in your organization that might be having a negative impact on the performance of the team or organization?

Here are some that I've heard over the years.

- You have to work late to get noticed around here.

- Once you've worked here for a certain number of years, no one can fire you.

- The leadership team doesn't know what they are doing.

- Our product isn't good.

- What I do doesn't really matter anyway.

- If you take vacation you might as well start looking for a new job.

- If you rock the boat you'll get fired.

What thoughts can you identify about your organization?
Write them down here.

Thoughts that exist within organization:

1._____

2._____

3._____

4._____

5._____

Now, take one of those thoughts and do the Self-Coaching
work on it here.

C= _____

T= _____

F= _____

A= _____

R= _____

What did you find out? What do you know now? I'm hoping you can see how an organizational thought really impacts the overall success of the business.

Let's try reworking it. With the circumstance remaining the same, see what might happen if you change the thought.

C= _____

T= _____

F= _____

A= _____

R= _____

You can do the same exercise now with your team. What thoughts or beliefs does your team have that might be impacting performance?

Again, here are a few examples:
- We don't have enough resources.
- We don't get paid enough for the work we do.
- Our boss doesn't listen to us.
- My boss should do a better job developing me.
- It's so and so's fault that we never hit our goals.
- The goals are too high.

Think about your team. What thoughts do you believe exist within your group? List them here.

1._____

2._____

3._____

4._____

5._____

What did you find out? What do you know now? I'm hoping you can see how a team thought impacts the overall success of the business.

> *Let's try reworking it. With the circumstance remaining the same, see what might happen if you change the thought.*
>
> *Now, take one of those thoughts and do Self-Coaching.*
>
> **C=** _____
>
> **T=** _____
>
> **F=** _____
>
> **A=** _____
>
> **R=** _____

The question that I'm sure you are now thinking is "what do I do now that I know all of this?" There are ineffective or destructive thoughts and beliefs that both my organization and my team believe that are affecting our ability to thrive as much as we could. How do I change that? What can I do to move my company's belief system?

I believe there are a few things that you can do to work through this and help others.

1. **Recognize whether or not you also believe the thought. If you do, do *Self-Coaching* on your thoughts. How does believing XYZ thought about your company affect you and your behavior? This work will first and foremost**

always be about you. So do your own work before you ever expect someone or something (like a big organization) to change.

2. **Recognize what you control.** We all have a space around us where we can immediately impact our environment. If you are a leader, you have the ability to impact those immediately around you.

   a. In the example I gave of the organization whose performance dramatically dropped, there were examples of teams whose performance did not change. In fact, there were teams that actually outperformed themselves. That difference in outcome had everything to do with the leader insulating the team members from the 'organizational belief' that paralyzed everyone else. Leaders make a tremendous impact on their team.

3. **Don't get caught up in group think.** Often referred to as water-cooler chat, right? If you are in it, you get what you get. If you stay out of it, you also get what you get. By managing your mind and what you allow into it, you also can see tremendously different results than those other leaders and managers around you. If you don't get caught in the fray of organizational or team beliefs, your team is likely to stay out of it as well.

THE PRIMARY QUESTION

I previously introduced the Primary Question as a thought in the form of a question that you ponder and play in your mind *repetitively*. This applies to all aspects of our lives: in our home life, our relationships, ourselves, and our work. The primary questions

I'm concerned with are the ones that have a negative impact on performance and results. As managers and leaders (who serve as coaches) we need to pay attention to what tape we are playing consistently in our minds—repetitive questions we ask ourselves, daily. Again, the best way to provide evidence for the primary question's relevance is through example.

Let's start with one that isn't about coaching, but is likely one that many on your team either think or have thought. If you've ever had a new job or worked in a new industry, you've had that aching feeling that you should know more than you know. It's that 'first-six-months-on-the-job' feeling where you constantly question what peoples' names are, let alone products, processes, etc. It's likely that people in these situations have a Primary Question that may be "why can't I figure this place out?" or "why can't I just get it?" I've heard people with questions like "is this job really for me?" or "can I really be successful in this kind of environment?"

I remember in my very first job I had a boss who was evil. Really she was ☺... nonetheless, every day I asked myself "why is she so mean?" Good news (not really) is that every day I found evidence to prove why she was mean, to me. I also found other people who thought she was mean. So, with me plugging along in my 21 year old self, believing my boss was mean AND finding constant evidence that she was mean what do you think happened?

Well, let me tell you, check it out.

Circumstance:	**Worked for a woman**
Thought:	**She is mean**
Feelings:	**Scared, worried, frightened**
Action:	**Timid, made mistakes, couldn't speak clearly**
Results:	**She got frustrated with her timid, mistake-making and inept speaking employee.**

What other questions do you think are out there in
Employee-land?

- **Why can't I get ahead?**
- **Why can't I figure out this process?**
- **Why can't I be more detail oriented?**
- **Why can't I multi-task?**
- **Why can't I be a better leader/boss/manager/coach?**
- **Why don't my people respect me?**
- **Why doesn't my team do what I tell them?**
- **Why don't people in this organization respect me?**
- **Why am I such a bad manager?**
- **And so on and so on and so on..**

Here's the fabulous news; we all have a Primary Question. If that Primary Question can have a negative answer AND generates further evidence to believe a junky thought, then it's time to shine some light on it and move it along.

What questions do you ask yourself on a regular basis?

_____

_____

_____

_____

The *answers* to the questions you ask are thoughts that you believe.

For example: **Why can't I lead a high performing team?**

- *Because I'm not a good leader.*
- *People don't respect me.*
- *My boss doesn't let me hire the right people.*

What thoughts are derived from the questions you ask yourself?

_____

_____

_____

_____

Put one of the thoughts in the model:

C: _____

T: _____

F: _____

A: _____

R: _____

By identifying the icky questions we ask ourselves, we can notice the thoughts that lead to poor results. When we *consciously* create a Primary Question we can intentionally create thoughts that support it.

For example: **How will I create a high performing team today?**

- *I will engage with each team member.*
- *I know the steps to take to reinforce excellent work.*
- *I am the model of what I want my team to be*

What Primary Question can you create today?

_____

_____

What thoughts support this question?

_____

_____

_____

_____

_____

_____

_____

Put one of the thoughts in the model:

C: _____

T: _____

F: _____

A: _____

R: _____

Most people's primary questions are pretty simple.

Here are a few I've heard from managers.

- **Will they figure out I really don't know what I'm doing?**
- **Why doesn't my team like me?**
- **Why doesn't anyone respect me?**
- **Why am I so unhappy in my job?**

There was a time in my professional life that I was struggling. It happens to the best of us, right? I was really unhappy, every day. I was unhappy because I was not managing my thoughts. I went from noticing what I was thinking, to actually believing what I was thinking. I forgot that believing my thoughts was optional. After a bit of tough coaching, I realized I was asking myself a really painful question everyday:

"Why is this happening to me?" – ICK!!

I found all sorts of evidence to explain why "this" was happening to me.

The answers looked like this:

- *Because you are stupid.*
- *Because you really never earned what you have anyway.*
- *Because they don't respect you.*
- *Because you aren't worth the success you have.*
- *Because you always lose what you have (ewwww!!).*

So, after I'd had enough, I did my own self-coaching. I focused on what I wanted in my life. I was resolved to find my own way and stop waiting for someone else to figure it out. I changed my Primary Question to:

"How can I create my own future today?"

This drove answers like these:

- *By focusing on what you love to do*
- *By finishing your book*
- *By surrounding yourself with like-minded, strong capable leaders*
- *By managing my thoughts*
- *By taking one step at a time*

It may seem obvious, but amazing things started to happen for me after I changed my primary question. No longer was I focusing on my junky thoughts that were the result of the totally ineffective question I was asking myself. By focusing on empowering, emboldening thoughts that stemmed from a new primary question, I changed my life. I'm not exaggerating. Seriously, take a minute and really think about what you are asking yourself, every day. You might be surprised to realize that much of what you are actualizing in your life and work, stems from the questions you ask yourself.

For the next thirty days, identify one new Primary Question you can ask yourself daily.

"Great minds have purpose, others have wishes."
~ Washington Irving

5

LEADERSHIP PURPOSE

W hat is your leadership purpose? Working with leaders this is probably one of my favorite topics to discuss. When I ask people what their leadership purpose is, I find the answers are tremendously mixed. It's a beautiful and fascinating thing. There's no right or wrong in the answer, But having AN answer is key to successful leadership. What's most important about your purpose is that you are connected to the fact that you have one. We all do.

The sooner you get clear about what your purpose is, what your reason is for doing the work you do, the sooner you'll be able to best direct your own career and the coaching you bring to everyone that joins you on your journey. When you are clear about what you are trying to achieve, it is easier to work with you, and it is actually easier to follow you and share in your journey. Why is that? Because when you are clear, you attract others who want to share in your purpose. They will be drawn to you. It's not by happenstance that like-driven people find one another.

Having clarity of purpose also directs your intention and keeps you clear about your decisions and direction. If you know where you are going and what you are trying to achieve it becomes clear when you should to say 'yes' or 'no' to a situation, a process, or a person. As a leader, this ability lends itself to clarity of decision making. It also makes coaching much easier. You have a point of view in your coaching, which comes from your purpose, which comes from your experience and inputs. When you coach from a clear point of view, you are consistent, unemotional, and thoughtful about how you approach your employees. When you don't have purpose, you are unclear, lack consistency, and lose your focus depending on the demands of your organization, team, etc.

Your experiences help you formulate who you are and what you want to achieve. Many people believe that experience predetermines destiny. I disagree. I believe that we have to look at our experiences to understand why we've made the choices we've made, but YOU get to decide where you are going. Nothing is predetermined. I think it's a brilliant gift to realize that you manage where you are going by connecting to your purpose. Bill George calls it your True North. Martha Beck calls it your North Star. All that you have behind you gives you information about who you are, but experiences of the past do not determine outcomes of the future.

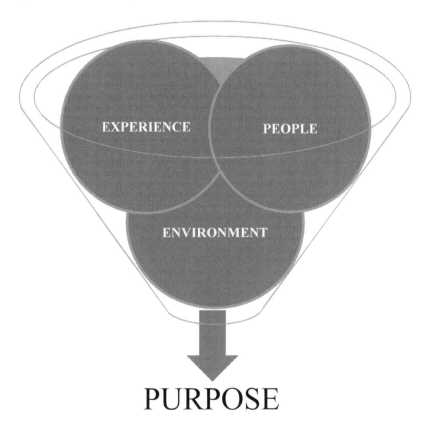

Over the course of your life, you have had countless experiences and interactions with people, places and things. All of those experiences get translated by your mind into meaning through stories. Stories create meaning of those events about a people, places or things. That's why we can all 'technically' have the same experience (a plane ride, sitting in a training workshop, working for the same boss) but create totally different meanings during the same experience. Our thoughts create stories about our experiences.

For example:
- *The plane ride was really turbulent. – Or -- That was one of the smoothest flights I've had in a long time.*
- *This workshop is tediously long. – Or -- This is the most riveting workshop I've ever attended.*
- *My boss is awesome. – Or -- My boss is a jerk.*

What's different? Your perspective, your experience, your story.

What does this have to do with leadership purpose? Based on the people, places and things you've encountered and the stories you've cultivated, you have started to define your purpose. What are you here for? What stories affect you the most? What do you bring into your work? The stories you bring into your work, shape HOW you show up as a leader and ultimately as a coach. It doesn't make any or all of those people, places, and things good or bad. They are "just." That's all.

What's important as we begin to explore ourselves as leaders and coaches is that we see that those stories have become filters and lenses that we use to interpret our life experiences, especially those at work. We use those filters and lenses to interpret what's happening around us within our organization with our team and consequently that all shows up in our decision making, leading and coaching.

When you feel passionately, you have evidence about your purpose. You have thoughts that are driving you toward achieving your goal.   Purpose is why people volunteer at particular organizations. Purpose is a culmination of a broad spectrum of exposure in your life, which shows up in who you are as a leader.

I went through a leadership workshop awhile back. It was in this workshop I realized I had a purpose. I was in a class of about twelve other people about eight years ago, and we were reviewing our personality profiles.   As we reviewed our results, we had to write down our primary goal or mission. I'll never forget writing:

"I want to challenge the way others think."

It has become my bumper sticker. It is my purpose. What's really cool about having written that down so many years ago, is that clarity has supported my decision making ever since.   While many people strive for senior leadership roles because of the monetary gain or the control, I choose it for the influence. The more people on my team, the greater my reach and scope. The more minds I can challenge to think differently. I love it. It doesn't mean they have to agree with my thinking, it just means I want an opportunity to challenge their unnoticed thinking. This purpose is why I coach and why I am so passionate about teaching others to coach. To me, helping others see there is another way, there is a way out and up, is a freeing gift. It is a gift I've had to learn, to practice, and now I want to give it away and back to others.

When I look at the people, places, and things in my life, it's clear to me why I have cultivated this purpose. I have had people in my life who suffer needlessly because of their thoughts. There are others in my life who have taught me how to step out of the mire of my thinking to find what is true. I've been exposed to a broad group of people and lived in several places. My curiosity in others saved me more times than I can say. Being inquisitive and genuinely interested in someone else is the surest way to disarm them. Trust me on that one. When you are new to a place or environment, asking questions is the best way to get the information you need. No assumptions, always ask. So, my combination of moving around, facing new and challenging situations, and watching strength and pain in those I love, has led me to this purpose. How I manifest it continues to be mine to own. But, I can hear her softly speaking to me, every day. When I challenge others to think differently, I win and frankly, so do they.

It is from this point of view and from my purpose of challenging other people's "think" that I coach. So, if you were to have a coaching conversation with me, you'd find I'd ask you a lot of questions, I'd be genuinely interested in what you say, and I would hear not only your words, but also your meaning. At some point in the conversation I would ask you some pointed questions based on your meaning, rather than your words to challenge your perspective and ask that you see another way. I believe it is why people have enjoyed working with and for me. It isn't that what I do is so fabulous, it has the impact because it is coming from my authentic, purposeful self, and others can feeeeel that.

This is a time for you to explore how your past and the inputs you've had are showing up in who you are today, especially as a leader. Thinking about your experiences through people, places, and things, and also exploring those things that are most important to you, will give you a window into your purpose.

Take a few minutes to reflect on the following questions.

Influences on who I am as a leader:

- **People**

  _____

  _____

  (continued)

- What stories / impact have they had on who I am as leader?

  _____

- Places

  _____

  _____

- What has been the impact of these places on my leadership?

  _____

  _____

- What have my experiences been that have influenced my leadership?

  _____

- What are the things that are most important to me as a leader?

  _____

- What do I want people to remember about me? What is my legacy?

  _____

- What am I most passionate about?

  _____

- What do I think about? What makes me unique?

  _____

I learned long ago, from a great leader, Vicki Merrill of DSAMIH Consulting, if you want something to stick, you've got to get it to a bumper sticker. Taking all the reflecting you've just done let's sum it all up into a purpose. So, what is it? Do you have some clarity?

Why not take a stab at it.

My leadership purpose is

_____

_____

_____

One of two things will happen. You either just totally nailed it and you're done or you will need to keep massaging your bumper sticker until it feels right. No matter. What's significant is that you are closer to establishing the rudder that will keep your leadership boat afloat for years to come. Your clarity is the key. From there we can continue more fabulous work together.

LEADERSHIP PURPOSE AND YOU AS COACH

I told you that my purpose is to challenge the way that others think. So, what do I do if someone doesn't want to think differently or worse yet, has absolutely no interest in even addressing the way they think about something? Well, trust me, this happens. Actually, it happens often, but I generally choose not to perseverate on those situations. However, it can and has been a block in my coaching.

Let's go back to the Self-Coaching Model.

Circumstance	Coaching Sue
Thought	Sue is stubborn and unwilling to change.
Feeling	Frustrated, angry, bothered, annoyed
Actions	Stop talking to Sue, avoid meetings with Sue
Results	Who's being stubborn? *(That'd be me. I'm the one who's annoyed that she won't play my game.)* Relationship with Sue doesn't improve, and I'm not helping Sue think differently, that's for sure.

Purpose is powerful. When we notice that we are feeling particularly frustrated with someone, it is incumbent upon us as coaches to understand why that may be the case and what we believe about the situation to create that frustration. Just because my purpose is to challenge other peoples' thinking, doesn't mean that everyone I meet shares my purpose. The people that want to know me, learn from me, gain insight from me, will. The people that have no interest in me, won't. But I don't get to say that Sue is stubborn and unwilling to change and use that as excuse to not coach and develop her. I still have to have my meetings with her and determine the best way to help her grow.

Here's the new thought I have about Sue.

Circumstance	Coaching Sue
Thought	I am learning from Sue.
Feeling	Interested
Actions	Meet with Sue; focus on her needs instead of mine.
Results	Sue feels listened to, I learn.

Let's say your purpose, for example, is to make a ton money. Maybe you want to get to be a CEO because you want to earn $550,000 per year by the time you are 45. That's awesome, go for it. I'm suggesting you check it when you are coaching others, because your purpose is likely showing up in your coaching.

Your purpose is not the same as other people's purposes. If you coached me, and tied everything we discussed back to earning potential and salary, you'd lose me. I'm not focused on that. Doesn't mean I don't want it. It just means I don't need to be coached from that point of view. That one is yours. Understanding this piece of who you are as a leader is so important. Having the awareness to know what is your purpose, but also to be able to hold that of your employees separate, helps you coach and development them authentically. Rather than needing everyone to want what you want, you can hear and see and understand each of them.

Your leadership purpose is that defining component of your leadership approach and personality. It is my hope your work in discovering and solidifying your purpose, will help you gain even further insight into your coaching approach. I hope that you see how you may have been unknowingly influencing your coaching conversations and focus with your team. Your purpose is present and you've been building teams around you that foster that purpose. Awareness allows you to now further advance that purpose and more effectively coach and lead, with clarity.

"The greatest good you can do for another is not just share your riches,
but to reveal to him, his own."
~ Benjamin Disraeli

6

COACHING OTHERS WITH *CHANGE YOUR THINK*

*D*on't be a 'fixer.'
I promised you at the beginning of this book that you would spend the majority of the time working on yourself. I think we've exhausted that. At this point, I'd like to help you apply what we've been learning to your team. I'm sure that as you've been doing this work, you've also been noticing and reflecting on the 'thoughts' of others. You can't help but not to do it. Once you start recognizing the difference between a circumstance and the thoughts about the circumstance, you start to *hear* them all over the place. As a result, it's also likely that you'll want to start telling people that they're just having 'thoughts' and they should change them! Most people get really enthusiastic about this tool, but the truth is that it only is effective when you live it yourself, then you can give it away with confidence and grace in the process. So, let's walk through some steps to introducing this to the team and how you, as coach, can begin to integrate the methods.

First, it's always good to let your team know that you've learned a new coaching method that you will be integrating into your conversations. I'm also a fan of a collaborative effort, so there's real value in sharing the learning with them as you go along. If you start having different conversations with them, they may wonder who you are and what you did with their boss. You can tell them that you've learned how thoughts may be impacting our ability to be successful in our roles. As a result, you will be working with them to determine what they you make particular situations *mean* and see if there is another way to think about a particular situation in your work. Because we all have different thoughts about situations, it's important to sometimes stop and reflect on those thoughts. Many times, our thoughts can be the key to why we aren't moving forward.

This would also be a really good time for you to share some of your own 'aha' moments as you've read through this book. Give them some examples of beliefs you had and worked on. Explain that you now see how they may have been impacting how well you perform in your role, in your work, or in your life. The great thing is that teaching is the best way to learn. So as you teach your team, you will be solidifying your learning and confidence with this model.

As a manager your employees' experience and perspective runs the gamut, I'm sure. You probably have folks on your team that are star teammates; they are your 'go to folks.' They are driven and ambitious and focus hard on their work. They own their performance; they know if success is to be theirs, it is up to them to deliver. The other side of that spectrum are teammates who find excuses for not performing and meeting goals. They blame their failures on others or on the market or on the product, etc. There are folks who wait to be told what to do and others who figure it out without much direction. Regardless of the players on your team, everyone has beliefs that 'limit' their abilities to achieve greater success. As you become comfortable with the *Self-Coaching Model*, you'll become a keen observer of others' limited thinking. The method of deconstructing Circumstances, Thoughts, Feelings, Actions, and Results gives you the structure to help others 'see' what they cannot on their own. As you notice these limiting thoughts, you'll start to make connections as to why someone may be stuck or unmotivated, or generally unsuccessful. As a manager to each person, using this tool allows you to have uniquely brilliant conversations with each member of your team. No coaching conversation will ever be the same because you will be working through each person's limited thinking as they are experiencing it.

As managers, we often start to 'lump' our employees into categories. Especially as it relates to performance and especially if you've been managing for a long time. Your experience weighs in quickly and you can make the dreaded ASSUMPTIONS. For example, if I tell you that someone on a team isn't doing well because he believes that the company doesn't provide enough resources for him to do his job, do you think of someone you've known in your past who's said that? Or what about someone who says that they could be successful if only the (name your department) would be more efficient, available, etc. We all do this. We all have managed long enough that we believe we know how to 'fix' an employee and/or their situation.

Since we've heard it all before, we immediately begin addressing their challenge with a solution. We 'fix' them. In fact, many of us are drawn to management because we can 'fix.' We have the control and authority to do so. But what happens when we 'fix?' What goes missing?

What we miss is the opportunity for a few things.

- **We don't develop our employees and help them find new solutions on their own.**
- **We make assumptions about the issue and provide a remedy that isn't really relevant.**
- **We don't help our employees see that the majority of what is going on is that they believe their own thoughts.**

Until they can start to recognize their contribution to the situation, they will not grow. In fact, they'll probably continue to face similar situations because they aren't learning about themselves in the process.

So why do managers default to fixing? 'Cause, it's EASY! If I can just tell you what to do, you'll be out of my office in fewer than five minutes. If I actually have to help you figure something out, especially support your development with *Self-Coaching* that's going to take waaaaaayyy more time and many managers find that to be a big, fat drag.

I know we work in a fast paced work environment. But if you were a home builder would you start with the roof? No, you'd have to build a solid foundation underneath the frame in order to have a stable, strong home. The same is true of our employees. While it may sure be easier just to tell someone how to address, fix, or resolve a problem or challenge, all you are doing is telling them how *you* would do it or how *you* did it. And you're telling them that from your experience, from your beliefs and from your perspective. You're not helping them with their foundation, their development.

If coaching is understanding others' intentions, then by telling and fixing we completely skip over the chance to understand another person's mind. The circumstance may seem totally alike, but the reasons for the situation and the thoughts behind it are totally unique. We all make similar circumstances 'mean' something totally different. You owe it to your employees to notice them and their thoughts before you begin advising and fixing. Right?

The other reason many managers like to 'fix' is because it makes them feel important and valuable. If I can tell you what to do to make your situation better, than I've added value to you. I'm 'worthy' of the manager title, right? Many people come into manager roles because they were good at what they used to do. So good in fact, it got them promoted. But often times folks get into management positions and realize they are not as good at the management stuff (maybe they don't even like it), as they were at the individual contribution stuff. As a result, they linger too long in the employee role. They focus on the work of the employee rather than the work of a manager.

Telling or fixing is sometimes a symptom of someone who isn't comfortable in their management role.   Subsequently, they continue to solve the employees' problems because it keeps them close to the action of the role and they know that role really well. The management role is less predictable, less clear.

So how do you know if you are a 'fixer'? Here are some questions to help you unravel the question:

When an employee comes to you with a problem or challenge, what do you do? Do you ask them questions and then ask them what solutions they have? Or do you start to tell them what they can do to resolve the issue? Think of the last time you were meeting with an employee who had a challenge. Replay that conversation in your mind. Be honest with yourself. Did you listen to them and help them find their own solution? Or did you take it on, come up with the solution, and tell them how to execute it?

If you are a fixer... time to do some 'thinking.'

Why do you want to fix?

_____

_____

_____

_____

_____

For example:

I want to fix employees' situation because I know how to do it the best way. And that way they won't create a mess I have to clean up.

(continued)

- **When you think this way, how do you *Feel*?**
  Irritated, annoyed
- **When you are irritated and annoyed how do you *Act*?**
  I'm in a hurry. I tell people what to do, quickly.
- **When you are in a hurry and tell your employees what to do, what kind of *Results* do you get?**
  They keep coming to me and asking me to fix their problems.

Aha! And so the pattern continues. In this example, employees not only come to their manager for solutions, they've come to *depend* on their manager for solutions. This would be a great example of the manager who goes to a conference for a day and has to check in with the team once every hour. The team is paralyzed when the manager isn't there because they have not been taught or allowed to think; the manager has to be involved in most decisions. As a result, employees have not been held accountable for their own performance and decisions. Interesting.

So, back to what you wrote about why you choose to 'fix' situations with your employees.

Let's complete the rest of the exercise.

I like to fix situations my employees are facing because

_____

_____

And when I believe this *Thought*, I *Feel*

_____

And when I *Feel* this way, I *Act*,

_____

(continued)

> **And when I *Act* this way, the *Results* I get are**
>
> _____
>
> _____

This provides more self-awareness for you. Hopefully, this is helping you see how your employees have stories that you attempt to "fix" in your role as manager. With your knowledge of the *Self-Coaching Model*, you'll be better armed now to help them see what they believe and how it is impacting their overall success.

One last word on managers who 'fix.' When you tell someone how to solve a problem, who owns the result? For example, suppose you and another employee, Debbie, aren't communicating frequently enough and it's causing a breakdown in the completion of projects. As your manager, I tell you to go talk to Debbie and suggest you tell her that you want to start a formal meeting with her weekly. You go talk with her and she shuts you down. She says she's just too busy and doesn't have any time on her calendar to meet with you right now. What do you think might come next? Whose fault is it that that idea didn't work? Often times it's the manager's fault! When you provide the "fix-it" idea, you own the failure. The employee can come right back to you and say, "I tried your idea and it didn't work. What else do you suggest?"

There's no doubt that anyone who's been a manager has had an employee come back and blame them for their failed performance. This is a classic case of passing accountability along to someone else. If your goal is to improve team accountability, one of the surest ways to do so is to help your employees find their own solutions, by 'hearing' their own thoughts, resolving to find new ones, and acting from a different feeling place. When they achieve results on their own, authentically, they will actually start to thank you. What's fascinating is YOU won't have done anything. It's brilliant.

YOU AND YOUR CURIOUS MIND

One thing I've found to be true of all the effective coaches I've known: they are all really curious about other people— genuinely. Curiosity born out of authentic interest can spark amazing mutual insight, especially between a coach and a coachee. So I ask you (out of curiosity) are you curious? Do you enjoy learning about other people? Do you listen intently to what people say and what they don't say? Do you 'hear' them say things that they aren't even hearing in themselves?

I think that authentic curiosity is a natural human tendency. It seems that we've needed it over the ages to help us understand our world. It's driven legions of scientists and explorers to further their knowledge. It helps us get to know people we fall in love with. It helps us make friends. So, curiosity isn't something that is new to us. It is an integral part of who we are. As a coach it is your primary tool when supporting others in their own development. Your curiosity helps them figure themselves out. When you are curious, you ask questions. And when you ask questions you explore information at a deeper level. It is through those questions that you find information that helps someone else see what they can't or choose not to see.

One of the other things I hold true about coaching is that every person is 'whole' onto themselves. It isn't the coach's job to put them back together or to give them their wisdom. Every person has their own wisdom, their own inner voice that knows exactly what they are supposed to be doing. So as a coach, you can take the pressure off of yourself to be the one that finds the answer. It's not your job. Your job is to help the people you are coaching find their own answers. And you do that best when you bring your curious mind into your conversations—every day.

What does curiosity look like in a coaching conversation? There are certainly plenty of books out there that can offer good coaching questions. I'm not a fan of such advice, only because I believe the questions have to come from a place of authenticity and you can't read that in a book. You have to listen to another person and build off of what they are telling you. Curiosity is work. It isn't just random questions out of a book. Curiosity is paying attention to the words, the sounds and inflections, the body language, their story. It's hearing patterns of stories or tendencies. It's understanding the people you work with well enough to notice them in ways that others don't. From that place, you can help them see what they don't.

Let me give you an example.

> *Just the other day I was talking with a manager; let's call him George. George was sharing with me his most recent coaching conversation with one of his employees, Julie. Julie had not followed up with a significant number of customers, so George expressed concern to Julie about her time management and urgency around her customer follow through. Julie responded that there was just too much work to do and she couldn't get to all of the customers assigned to her. At that point in the conversation, George decided to show Julie a report that outlined how much time she was actually working on customer issues and support. The report showed that she was not spending as much time working with customers as she said she was.*
>
> *After George told me about the customer service time report he showed her, I asked him what happened next. He said she agreed she needed to work harder and that she would get right to it. The coaching conversation between Julie and George ended. George believes that Julie will get the work done. Do you?*
>
> (continued)

> *As I was listening to George I heard a few things. I heard George as frustrated. I could hear it in his voice. It was clearly not the first time he'd talked with this employee about her customer service follow through. I also thought of him showing this employee a report that documented the number of hours she had worked with customers sort of interesting. It just didn't seem to fit into the context of the conversation. It seemed kind of "gotcha management-ish."*
>
> *I asked George, "What were you thinking about this employee before you met with her?"*
>
> *He replied, "She is going to try and manipulate me."*

Interesting. So, in preparation of her 'manipulation,' George ran a report that documented hours worked so she wouldn't be able to use that excuse.

Circumstance:	Not proper customer follow up
Thought:	She's going to manipulate me.
Feeling:	Frustrated
Actions:	Ran reports but didn't show them until she had given her answers.
Results:	George manipulated the conversation with Julie by not sharing the info up front. The situation stays the same.

> *Even more interesting. I asked him how many times he has had a conversation like that with her. He said numerous times. Even MORE interesting! They've had this conversation numerous times. He tries to "catch" her by showing her a report that says she isn't really trying to work hard. She backs down and says she'll do the work. She doesn't do the work and he has the same conversation with her next week.*

(continued)

How effective is this coaching relationship? Not very. How well are they supporting their customers? Not very. So the manager's thought that the employee will manipulate him, makes him angry. He runs reports to prove her wrong and then the repeat button gets pushed. In the meantime, the customers are not getting proper follow-up.

Ultimately, George realized that because he was focused on his story about this employee, he wasn't taking care of the customer or truly holding Julie accountable for failed service; rather he was trying to prove Julie wrong. Once he realized this, he started focusing on how best to support his customers. He could reassign them, etc. He let go of his story about Julie and redirected his focus.

Julie could stop playing the sit-there-and-take-it game. If he took those customers away because she wasn't following up with them, she would stand to lose. He was better able to hold accountability when he lost the story and changed his thought.

Circumstance:	**Not proper customer follow up**
Thought:	**I will ensure the customers are handled properly.**
Feeling:	**Empowered**
Actions:	**Assign customers to people who will support them.**
Results:	**Ends game between George and Julie. Customers get proper follow-up.**

Curiosity showed up for me in this conversation when he started talking about the report he ran to prove she really hadn't been working that hard. I thought to myself, "That's really interesting. I want to know more about that." In the space of curiosity the word "why" is the best go to. Asking people "why" they do what they do inevitably exposes their thoughts. Effective or ineffective, those tricky little thoughts will show themselves when you inquire with a "why" question. If you are authentically curious, then you can and will ask "why" a lot. It's like a vegetable peeler; it just keeps pulling back the layers until you get to the core of the story.

Using George as an example, believing his employee Julie is trying to manipulate him is a really cruddy thought. It will continue to drive him to focus on the wrong things related to her performance and to her success. Asking a few "why" questions helped him see what he believed and how that was impeding his ability to coach Julie and achieve business results.

WHAT *WHY* REVEALS

Asking "why" questions helps you as coach hear the story behind each employee's performance issues and other challenges. You can do this for practice with anyone. Next time you want to go out to dinner with a friend ask them what they want to eat. When they tell you, ask them why. Inevitably they'll tell you their thought.

> *"I'd like to have Mexican food."*
> *"Why?"*
> *"I don't know. I guess it just sounds good tonight."*
>   *(Thought)*
> *"Why does it sound good?"*
> *"I'm in kind of a hearty-meal kind of mood." (Thought)*
> *"Huh? Why's that?"*
> *"It's been a long day. I just want to give myself a treat, I*
>   *guess." (Thought)*

You could take this further if you wanted. Why do they need to give themselves a treat with food after a long day? That'd be an interesting question.

Here's another example.

> *"I really hope I don't have to work with Alvin on that project." (Thought)*
> *"Really, why?"*
> *"Because he always takes over." (Thought)*
> *"Why is that a problem for you?"*
> *"Because I want to be able to express my ideas too." (Thought)*
> *"Why does Alvin taking over mean you can't express your ideas?"*
> *"Well, I guess it doesn't. It's just a drag when nobody listens to me." (BIG FAT UGLY THOUGHT!)*

So, this person only wants to play with people *he* thinks are listening to him. That's interesting, don't you think? Can you see how the project with Alvin is doomed from the start and how it's very likely that he will, in fact, take over?

As coach, your "why" questions help both you and your employee see how the thinking they have is affecting their ability to perform, manage relationships, and projects.

Sometimes at the day-to-day level, painful, limiting beliefs can create a tremendous struggle for our employees at work. You are able to help them find resolution and apply a new thought. As a result, you'll be supporting them, but you'll also be increasing the likelihood of organizational success.

Let's play this example out with Alvin if he were to apply Self-Coaching.

Circumstance:	**Working on a project with Alvin—why does that concern you?**
Thought:	*Because he won't listen to me.*

(continued)

Feeling: **So when you think that Alvin won't listen to you, how do you feel?**
Angry, hurt

Actions: **And when you are feeling angry and hurt, how do you act (especially around Alvin)?**
Withdrawn and quiet

Results: **Hmmm. So what kind of results do you get when you are withdrawn and quiet around Alvin?**
Is it likely Alvin won't listen to me because I won't say anything!

New thought, same circumstance:

Circumstance: **Working on a project with Alvin—why does that concern you?**

Thought: **What's something else you can believe? (No made up stuff here—what can you really believe?)**
I believe I can speak my mind.

Feeling: **Great, so when you believe that you can speak your mind, how do you feel?**
Strong, interested

Actions: **And when you are feeling strong and interested how will you act (especially around Alvin)?**
Expressive

Results: **And so if you are acting expressive, what kind of results are you likely to get working on this project with Alvin.**
I speak up and contribute.

Which approach is more likely to get you the results you want??

A few little "why" questions and we were able to help this employee preempt a situation with Alvin that may have only served to further diminish his credibility and results. The other thing that's really cool about this tool is that people love you for it. They really, really appreciate the insight you help them gain into *themselves.* It doesn't take much, because like I said, we all have our own wisdom. But helping someone see that what they believe is the only thing preventing their results (and happiness) is a brilliant gift to give.

HOW DO I 'HEAR' THOUGHTS?

As a manager I can only imagine the limiting thoughts you hear from people on your team every day. When people learn this approach, one of the first things to do is to start 'listening' for limiting thoughts.

Those thoughts tend to start with phrases like:
- **"I can't"**
- **"I'm not"**
- **"I've never been"**
- **"No one will"**
- **"Everybody thinks"**
- **"He/she never"**
- **"It's just how I am"**
- **"He/she always"**

We all do this. We all have thoughts that are impeding our ability to achieve success, but the reasons are uniquely ours. They are based on our stories, not on someone else's. That's why as coach you have to develop the patience to question other people's thinking. When someone says "I can't do that. I'm just not good at it." That's a great opportunity for a "why" question.

Instead, what a lot of people do in that moment is appease their employees. They try to make them feel better. So, they start telling them all the reasons they are good (whatever it is). They look for evidence to disprove their story. But the problem is, no matter how much of *your* evidence you provide, it isn't *theirs*. Until someone can see that it's actually their story and their thoughts that are contributing to the failure or lack of confidence, they'll not break the cycle. It reminds me of a great quote I read the other day that unfortunately is from an unknown source, "I can believe in you, but I cannot believe for you."

"Why" questions catch people in their tracks. When they have to dig around and describe and explain statements like "I'm just not good at it," they have to really connect with what they mean. They have to explore it further. The more they are willing to connect to the story they believe, the more you can help them climb out of it.

As you are practicing this approach in your coaching conversations, it's important to take your time and listen to people for a while. Develop your ear for listening to people and what they make situations mean. I think you'll find that about 80% of the world we live in, the facts we mistakenly believe, are really just someone else's thoughts rolled up into stories.

The gift you bring to your employees and others that you coach is your ability to *discern* the difference. The more astute you become at isolating the facts out of a situation, especially as you are working with others, the more relevant your coaching becomes. When you can help others see what they cannot, you become a trusted and valuable part of the team. You become the person that your employees will confide and share with because they know you'll bring perspective and insight, which will lead them to a change.

Once you've helped employees see the thinking they have and how it is adversely impacting the results they seek, you help them deconstruct and find a better, more useful thought.

At first, many people tell me it feels kind of 'clunky' in a coaching conversation. Whipping out a *Self-Coaching* worksheet can seem a bit formal. That's why I really suggest doing this work on yourself before you begin practicing with others. Once you are comfortable with it, it really is conversational. It doesn't have to be a form that you fill in each blank line, but one that you teach them to capture.

As I outlined in the Alvin example, it's really just a series of questions you ask of your employee when they tell you about a circumstance, situation, or person.

For example, you can start off by asking them a few "Why" questions to get at the thought. From there, you follow the model.

- **When you believe that *Thought* how do you *Feel*?**

- **When you *Feel* _____ , how do you *Act*?**

- **When you *Act* _____ what *Results* do you get or are likely to get?**

- **Tie the *Results* back to the original *Thought*.**

So can you see that these results are supporting the originating thought? In order to help someone identify a new thought that leads to better or improved results, you can ask them a question like, "What's something else you can believe about this circumstance, situation, or person?"

- *Thought* _____

- **When you believe that *Thought* how do you *Feel*?**

- **When you are *Feeling* _____ how are you likely to *Act*?**

- **When you *Act*_____ what *Results* are you likely to get?**

Aha! Can you see how working on a new thought is more likely to support a new and better result?

Here is a blank Self-Coaching practice worksheet for you or your team.

Circumstance: _____

_____

When this happened, what did you make it mean?

Thought: _____

_____

When you believe this thought, how do you feel?

Feeling: _____

_____

When you feel this way, how do you act?

Actions: _____

_____

When you act this way, what results do you get?

Results: _____

_____

The thing is, the original thought will not go away. But creating a new thought that the mind can choose from helps train the brain to follow through with another plan. It doesn't have to believe the icky thought; it can believe another one that drives better feelings and ultimately better outcomes. If we get to pick our thoughts anyway, let's pick thoughts that make us feel good. We choose our thoughts, always.

As a coach, you can help your employees see how their thinking is creating their results. When this dialogue begins and becomes a consistent coaching method, things start to happen.

- **You develop your team.**
- **You teach them to notice themselves before they notice others.**
- **They recognize their accountability to the issues, challenges, and performance outcomes they are getting.**
- **They will also begin applying the coaching method to their life overall and they will thank you for it.**
- **You develop as a leader and as a coach because you get out of the way and learn how to help others grow, without always telling them what to do.**
- **It becomes a language of the team and everyone can catch each other when they believe a limiting thought.**

SO ONCE WE'VE COME UP WITH A NEW THOUGHT, THEN WHAT?

Once you've helped your employee identify a new thought it is important that the two of you develop a follow up strategy and plan to ensure they continue to focus on the new thought (which leads to new results). Most plans only focus on the result. There is importance in having your eye on the outcome, but we also want to acknowledge the value in 'getting there.' My suggestion is that you build a plan around both the result and around supporting the employee master and maintain their new thought so it becomes a part of who they are, rather than just a thing to get done.

Using the situation with Alvin again, the employee decided that his new thought would be "I can speak my mind." The result he is planning for is that he will contribute to the project he and Alvin are working on.

In follow up meetings with him we'd want to stay focused on those two things. For example:

- *What solutions did you offer during your last project meeting?*
- *What ideas did you contribute?*
- *How are you acting on the ideas that you have?*

Also, it's important to keep your curiosity hat on all the time with this employee. If he has a tendency to shut down around teammates that are assertive or boisterous, then it will be important for you to observe him in those situations and provide follow up feedback. If you see him shutting down in a meeting, ask him what was going on. Inquire how he was demonstrating "I can speak my mind." It's likely it will spark further stories from the employee and that's okay. If it has been a deeply held belief, then it will take a while to continue to unravel it.

I mentioned the concept of spider thoughts. Usually a thought doesn't live all on its own. It's connected to many other thoughts. Once you've uncovered the thought "I can't speak my mind," it's likely that there will be other supporting or more deeply rooted thoughts that exist.

- *I don't have anything important to say.*
- *People will think I'm dumb.*
- *I'm not prepared for my job.*
- *I'm not smart.*

These are just examples, but it can be a liberating way to help yourself and others understand how many thoughts they have that are impacting their performance in a particular area. You can brainstorm by listing the thoughts, that spring from one another, like I did above. Or sometimes it's helpful to draw them out in a map—starting with a thought in the center and then branching out additional thoughts that come up with a connecting line.

However you choose to do this work is up to you. What's important is that once a negative thought is identified, it's important to do the work on each one.

"Seeing" the thought is only half the experience. Following it through to find a more productive, better feeling thought is where the work really is.

Your awareness and attentiveness to this kind of employee development is so imperative. You are the objective one and you can notice (hear) his thoughts so much more than he can, especially when it is a pervasive blind spot.

Your follow up plan needs to be related to the results AND to the follow up observation where you are specifically working with the employee on where the limiting thought(s) are continuing to disrupt their performance.

Sample Follow Up Plan:

- **Employee will contribute two new ideas at each project team meeting.**

- **Development and implementation plan to be completed by XYZ date.**

- **Manager to provide further observation of employee during project team meetings to support development of new beliefs around the peer relationship.**

Think of it this way. As an organization you have to have outcome goals or activity goals. But you also have to have developmental goals for each employee. The Self-Coaching model supports you in the creation of those development goals.

One of the things an employee and I are working on is her lack of interest or her aversion, frankly, to networking and being forced to meet other leaders. To her it is not authentic and genuine and is counter to who she thinks she is. As a result, she avoids meeting and interacting with some leaders that would probably be helpful in the advancement of the team's goals and of her own career. We've been working on it for a while from a development perspective.   The development conversation centers on the Self-Coaching model. I ask her a lot of "why" questions to help us understand what she makes situations mean. It has helped us get a clear perspective of the story and also helped her see how those beliefs are impeding her ability to succeed in building some new relationships.

There have been times where we've creating some activity goals and she is working on her thoughts, but she also has work that needs to get done. Because she knows that I understand her challenge, it makes it a lot easier for us to set intermediary activity goals that support her long term development. For example, when we were at a large conference, I suggested she go meet two leaders she didn't know. She grumbled and groaned about it, but we also both know that the thought she has around this activity is detrimental and a lie. So, she can't dodge the goal. But she does have to notice herself first and then move forward. We talked about how this activity will help her in her long term goal.

Using the *Self-Coaching Model* is not a way for employees to avoid accountability, it is the exact opposite. It is a brilliant way for you both to understand the underlying thoughts that are creating the   challenge,   but   then   to   continue   to   move   the results/business/organization   forward   in   the   employee's development.

"Excellence is not a singular act, but a habit.
You are what you repeatedly do."
~ Shaquille O'Neil

7

PUTTING IT ALL TOGETHER

Once you've practiced the *Self-Coaching Model* enough with your own challenges, you will feel ready to integrate it into coaching with your team.

Here are the steps to follow.

1. **Tell your team you have learned a new coaching methodology, and you will be working with them to discern how what they believe, is actually driving the results they are getting.**

2. **Start listening to the limiting thoughts of your team before you do anything. Write down common thoughts you hear that you can tie back to poor outcomes. Make note of any patterns or consistencies of thought—either with individuals or with the team as a whole.**

3. **Teach them the model. Pull them all into a meeting room and outline the *Self-Coaching Model*.**

4. **Help them understand the "*Why*" before you begin applying the model.**

5. **When someone says "*I can't*" or any of the other statements that indicate a limiting thought, ask "*Why*"**

questions to further understand what the overall story is and what the underlying thought is.

6. Walk your employees through the model to help them see how their current thoughts are limiting their results. Take them through the process of identifying new thoughts.

7. Build a plan with your employees to set goals around:

 a. New thoughts they've determined. How will they keep them top of mind?

 b. Performance goals that are tied to the expected new result(s).

 c. Anticipated outcomes of new thoughts?

 d. Evaluation procedures: How will the employees and you know that they are progressing?

"A conclusion is simply the place where someone got tired of thinking." ~
Unknown

8

FINAL THOUGHTS

I wrote this book because I know if you apply the concepts to your work as a manager-coach, you will achieve great results. I started applying these concepts with my team over six years ago and have seen consistent success in several ways. The teams I've led have all been recognized as top performing teams. I have little if no attrition from my direct reports. The people I have had and continue to have the opportunity to work with love what they do and we all enjoy spending our time together, each day. That is born out of an honesty and authenticity that can only come when you are aware of and manage your thinking. We all accept accountability for our contribution to each situation. There's something to be said for finding joy in your work. I've found it and I know that the Self-Coaching model has been a contributing factor to my joy in both leading and coaching.

There are many coaching philosophies available to us to study. I encourage managers at all levels to seek out new ideas and information as quickly as they can apply it. Learning and growing is not only intriguing, it is a responsibility of a manager. As you grow and challenge yourself to think differently, you are able to offer new ideas and solutions to your team. If you accept the notion that as a manager you have a significant opportunity to play a big part in your employees' lives, then you know the importance of self-development.

Self-awareness comes with your development. As you learn more, you see more. The more aware you are of your challenges and opportunities, the more of able you are to help others identify theirs.

My hope is that tools in this book have contributed to the life-long learning you will have in your leadership your career. As I mentioned, my leadership purpose is to challenge how and what people think. It is my hope that I have continued that purpose and helped you to "Change Your Think."

"Every end is a new beginning."
~ Proverb

APPENDIX

For more tools and resources, please go to www.krisplachy.com.

Steps to using the Self-Coaching Model:

- Identify your biggest coaching challenges.
- Tell the story of each challenge.
- Identify the facts.
- Identify the thoughts.
- Work through each thought using the *Self-Coaching Model.*
- Come up with an alternate model, using a new thought.
- Pay attention to yourself; recognize when you are feeling negative feelings.
- Do not coach or manage until you have determined what thoughts you believe about the employee or situation.
- Do this work daily… there are always new thoughts to uncover and deconstruct.

Top Managing/Coaching Challenges:

_____

_____

_____

_____

_____

_____

_____

Tell the story of the challenges:

_____

_____

_____

_____

_____

_____

_____

_____

_____

_____

_____

_____

_____

What are the facts? (Do this for each challenge.)

_____

_____

_____

_____

_____

_____

_____

_____

What are your thoughts? (Do this for each challenge.)

_____

_____

_____

_____

_____

_____

_____

_____

SELF-COACHING WORKSHEET

Circumstance: (must be provable fact)
(What happened?)

_____

_____

_____

What do you make that mean?

Thought: (sentence in your mind that you use to describe/define the circumstance)

_____

_____

_____

When you believe this thought, how do you feel?

Feeling: (a one word emotion descriptor)

_____

When you feel this way, how do you act?

Action: (actions/behaviors that you do)

_____

_____

_____

What results do you get when you act this way?

Results: (outcomes of actions/behaviors)

_____

_____

_____

SELF-COACHING WORKSHEET

Circumstance: (must be provable fact)
(What happened?)
_____

_____

_____

What do you make that mean?

Thought: (sentence in your mind that you use to describe/define
the circumstance)

_____

_____

_____

When you believe this thought, how do you feel?

Feeling: (a one word emotion descriptor)

_____

When you feel this way, how do you act?

Action: (actions/behaviors that you do)

_____

_____

_____

What results do you get when you act this way?

Results: (outcomes of actions/behaviors)

_____

_____

_____

SELF-COACHING WORKSHEET

Circumstance: (must be provable fact)
(What happened?)

_____

_____

_____

What do you make that mean?

Thought: (sentence in your mind that you use to describe/define
the circumstance)

_____

_____

_____

When you believe this thought, how do you feel?

Feeling: (a one word emotion descriptor)

_____

When you feel this way, how do you act?

Action: (actions/behaviors that you do)

_____

_____

_____

What results do you get when you act this way?

Results: (outcomes of actions/behaviors)

_____

_____

_____

SELF-COACHING WORKSHEET

Circumstance: (must be provable fact)
(What happened?)

_____

_____

_____

What do you make that mean?

Thought: (sentence in your mind that you use to describe/define the circumstance)

_____

_____

_____

When you believe this thought, how do you feel?

Feeling: (a one word emotion descriptor)

_____

When you feel this way, how do you act?

Action: (actions/behaviors that you do)

_____

_____

_____

What results do you get when you act this way?

Results: (outcomes of actions/behaviors)

_____

_____

_____

SELF-COACHING WORKSHEET

Circumstance:
(What happened?)

(must be provable fact)

_____

_____

_____

What do you make that mean?

Thought:

(sentence in your mind that you use to describe/define the circumstance)

_____

_____

_____

When you believe this thought, how do you feel?

Feeling:

(a one word emotion descriptor)

_____

When you feel this way, how do you act?

Action:

(actions/behaviors that you do)

_____

_____

What results do you get when you act this way?

Results:

(outcomes of actions/behaviors)

_____

_____

_____

SELF-COACHING WORKSHEET

Circumstance: (must be provable fact)
(What happened?)

_____

_____

_____

What do you make that mean?

Thought: (sentence in your mind that you use to describe/define the circumstance)

_____

_____

_____

When you believe this thought, how do you feel?

Feeling: (a one word emotion descriptor)

_____

When you feel this way, how do you act?

Action: (actions/behaviors that you do)

_____

_____

_____

What results do you get when you act this way?

Results: (outcomes of actions/behaviors)

_____

_____

_____

SELF-COACHING WORKSHEET

Circumstance: (must be provable fact)
(What happened?)

_____

_____

_____

What do you make that mean?

Thought: (sentence in your mind that you use to describe/define the circumstance)

_____

_____

_____

When you believe this thought, how do you feel?

Feeling: (a one word emotion descriptor)

_____

When you feel this way, how do you act?

Action: (actions/behaviors that you do)

_____

_____

_____

What results do you get when you act this way?

Results: (outcomes of actions/behaviors)

_____

_____

_____

SELF-COACHING WORKSHEET

Circumstance: (must be provable fact)
(What happened?)

_____

_____

_____

What do you make that mean?

Thought: (sentence in your mind that you use to describe/define the circumstance)

_____

_____

_____

When you believe this thought, how do you feel?

Feeling: (a one word emotion descriptor)

_____

When you feel this way, how do you act?

Action: (actions/behaviors that you do)

_____

_____

What results do you get when you act this way?

Results: (outcomes of actions/behaviors)

_____

_____

_____

SELF-COACHING WORKSHEET
REWORKING THOUGHTS

Circumstance: (must be provable fact)
(What happened?)

_____

_____

_____

What do you make that mean?

Thought: (sentence in your mind that you use to describe/define
the circumstance)

_____

_____

_____

*When you believe this thought, how do you
feel?*

Feeling: (a one word emotion descriptor)

_____

When you feel this way, how do you act?

Action: (actions/behaviors that you do)

_____

_____

_____

*What results do you get when you act this
way?*

Results: (outcomes of actions/behaviors)

_____

_____

SELF-COACHING WORKSHEET
REWORKING THOUGHTS

Circumstance: (must be provable fact)
(What happened?)
_____

_____

_____

What do you make that mean?

Thought: (sentence in your mind that you use to describe/define
the circumstance)

_____

_____

_____

When you believe this thought, how do you feel?

Feeling: (a one word emotion descriptor)

_____

When you feel this way, how do you act?

Action: (actions/behaviors that you do)

_____

_____

_____

What results do you get when you act this way?

Results: (outcomes of actions/behaviors)

_____

_____

SELF-COACHING WORKSHEET
REWORKING THOUGHTS

Circumstance: (must be provable fact)
(What happened?)

_____

_____

_____

What do you make that mean?

Thought: (sentence in your mind that you use to describe/define
the circumstance)

_____

_____

_____

When you believe this thought, how do you feel?

Feeling: (a one word emotion descriptor)

_____

When you feel this way, how do you act?

Action: (actions/behaviors that you do)

_____

_____

_____

What results do you get when you act this way?

Results: (outcomes of actions/behaviors)

_____

_____

SELF-COACHING WORKSHEET
REWORKING THOUGHTS

Circumstance: (must be provable fact)
(What happened?)

_____

_____

_____

What do you make that mean?

Thought: (sentence in your mind that you use to describe/define the circumstance)

_____

_____

_____

When you believe this thought, how do you feel?

Feeling: (a one word emotion descriptor)

_____

When you feel this way, how do you act?

Action: (actions/behaviors that you do)

_____

_____

_____

What results do you get when you act this way?

Results: (outcomes of actions/behaviors)

_____

_____

SELF-COACHING WORKSHEET
REWORKING THOUGHTS

Circumstance:　(must be provable fact)
(What happened?)

_____

_____

_____

What do you make that mean?

Thought:　(sentence in your mind that you use to describe/define
the circumstance)

_____

_____

_____

When you believe this thought, how do you feel?

Feeling:　(a one word emotion descriptor)

_____

When you feel this way, how do you act?

Action:　(actions/behaviors that you do)

_____

_____

What results do you get when you act this way?

Results:　(outcomes of actions/behaviors)

_____

_____

SELF-COACHING WORKSHEET
REWORKING THOUGHTS

Circumstance: (must be provable fact)
(What happened?)

_____

_____

_____

What do you make that mean?

Thought: (sentence in your mind that you use to describe/define the circumstance)

_____

_____

_____

When you believe this thought, how do you feel?

Feeling: (a one word emotion descriptor)

_____

When you feel this way, how do you act?

Action: (actions/behaviors that you do)

_____

_____

_____

What results do you get when you act this way?

Results: (outcomes of actions/behaviors)

_____

_____

SELF-COACHING WORKSHEET
REWORKING THOUGHTS

Circumstance: (must be provable fact)
(What happened?)

_____

_____

_____

What do you make that mean?

Thought: (sentence in your mind that you use to describe/define the circumstance)

_____

_____

_____

When you believe this thought, how do you feel?

Feeling: (a one word emotion descriptor)

_____

When you feel this way, how do you act?

Action: (actions/behaviors that you do)

_____

_____

_____

What results do you get when you act this way?

Results: (outcomes of actions/behaviors)

_____

_____

SELF-COACHING WORKSHEET
REWORKING THOUGHTS

Circumstance: (must be provable fact)
(What happened?)
_____

_____

_____

What do you make that mean?

Thought: (sentence in your mind that you use to describe/define
the circumstance)

_____

_____

_____

When you believe this thought, how do you feel?

Feeling: (a one word emotion descriptor)

_____

When you feel this way, how do you act?

Action: (actions/behaviors that you do)

_____

_____

_____

What results do you get when you act this way?

Results: (outcomes of actions/behaviors)

_____

_____

SELF-COACHING WORKSHEET
REWORKING THOUGHTS

Circumstance: (must be provable fact)
(What happened?)

_____

_____

_____

What do you make that mean?

Thought: (sentence in your mind that you use to describe/define the circumstance)

_____

_____

_____

When you believe this thought, how do you feel?

Feeling: (a one word emotion descriptor)

_____

When you feel this way, how do you act?

Action: (actions/behaviors that you do)

_____

_____

_____

What results do you get when you act this way?

Results: (outcomes of actions/behaviors)

_____

_____

SELF-COACHING WORKSHEET
REWORKING THOUGHTS

Circumstance: (must be provable fact)
(What happened?)

_____

_____

_____

What do you make that mean?

Thought: (sentence in your mind that you use to describe/define the circumstance)

_____

_____

When you believe this thought, how do you feel?

Feeling: (a one word emotion descriptor)

_____

When you feel this way, how do you act?

Action: (actions/behaviors that you do)

_____

_____

What results do you get when you act this way?

Results: (outcomes of actions/behaviors)

_____

_____

REWORKING THOUGHTS
STARTING WITH A FEELING

When I work with _____,

 I want to feeeeeel _____.

When I feeeeeeel _____

with _____,

I will act _____.

When I act _____

with _____

the results I will get are _____

_____.

Circumstance: Working with XYZ employee

> **Thought:** (new thought here)
>
> _____

> **Feeling:** (pull from worksheet above)
>
> _____

> **Actions:** (pull from worksheet above)
>
> _____

> **Results:** (pull from worksheet above)
>
> _____

REWORKING THOUGHTS
STARTING WITH A FEELING

When I work with _____,

 I want to feeeeeel _____.

When I feeeeeeel _____

with _____,

I will act _____.

When I act _____

with _____

the results I will get are _____

_____.

Circumstance: Working with XYZ employee

Thought: (new thought here)

_____

Feeling: (pull from worksheet above)

_____

Actions: (pull from worksheet above)

_____

Results: (pull from worksheet above)

_____

REWORKING THOUGHTS
STARTING WITH A FEELING

When I work with _____ ,

 I want to feeeeeel _____ .

When I feeeeeeel _____

with _____ ,

I will act _____ .

When I act _____

with _____

the results I will get are _____

_____ .

Circumstance: Working with XYZ employee

Thought: (new thought here)

_____

Feeling: (pull from worksheet above)

_____

Actions: (pull from worksheet above)

_____

Results: (pull from worksheet above)

_____

REWORKING THOUGHTS
STARTING WITH A FEELING

When I work with _____,

I want to feeeeeel _____.

When I feeeeeeel _____

with _____,

I will act _____.

When I act _____

with _____

the results I will get are _____

_____.

Circumstance: Working with XYZ employee

Thought: (new thought here)

_____

Feeling: (pull from worksheet above)

_____

Actions: (pull from worksheet above)

_____

Results: (pull from worksheet above)

_____

THOUGHTS ABOUT ACCOUNTABILITY

What is your belief about Accountability?

_____

_____

Why do you believe this?

_____

_____

Why? (rephrase thought above)

_____

_____

Why? (rephrase thought above)

_____

_____

Why?

_____

_____

Why?

_____

_____

RESULTS OF THOUGHTS ABOUT ACCOUNTABILITY

How does your *belief* about accountability affect or impact your coaching *others* on accountability?

_____

_____

_____

What potential roadblocks to holding others accountable may present themselves, based on your story and beliefs

_____

_____

_____

How is not holding accountability conversations affecting the performance of your team?

_____

_____

_____

How can you reframe your belief to have a positive effect on your outcomes?

_____

_____

_____

EXAMPLES OF THE SELF-COACHING MODEL IN ACTION

Circumstance: New manager replaced promoted director

Thought: She doesn't treat my team like I did

Feeling: Betrayed

Actions: Blunt, overly critical

Results: Not communicating well with new manager. Director is not treating his new manager like he used to treat his team.

Reworked thought:

Circumstance: New manager replaced promoted director

Thought: We are partners

Feeling: Confident

Actions: Coach, observe

Results: She improves as a manager. Director is treating his new manager like he used to treat his old team.

Circumstance:	Team not meeting performance expectations
Thought:	My employees should care as much as I do about our poor performance.
Feeling:	Anger, resentment
Actions:	Sleeplessness, short-tempered with team
Results:	No improved performance. Manager not caring about employees, only caring about performance.

Reworked thought:

Circumstance:	Team not meeting performance expectations
Thought:	The team's performance is my responsibility
Feeling:	Empowered
Actions:	Focus on specific performance gaps of each player
Results:	Improved team performance and team dynamic

Circumstance: Employee isn't meeting performance expectations

Thought: She gets defensive when I give her feedback.

Feeling: Annoyed

Actions: Avoid employee

Results: No feedback given. Manager is actually the one acting defensive because he doesn't like how the employee responds to his feedback.

Reworked thought:

Circumstance: Employee isn't meeting performance expectations.

Thought: I cannot predict the employee's response to feedback.

Feeling: Calm

Actions: Provide feedback

Results: Employee may or may not improve. Manager is properly providing performance feedback.

Circumstance: Manager takes over a new team

Thought: I got the bottom of the barrel employees

Feeling: Helpless

Actions: Find excuses for not helping them improve; don't coach

Results: Team's results continue to be poor

Reworked thought:

Circumstance: Manager takes over a new team

Thought: I know how to build a successful team.

Feeling: Resolved

Actions: Focused, coach and hold team accountable to performance

Results: Players either improve or leave; team becomes more successful.

KRIS PLACHY

KRIS PLACHY is a recognized, innovative Performance Coach specializing in a thoughtful coaching approach that allows companies and individuals to gain valuable insight into their performance. In addition to her Masters in Organizational Management, she is a Certified Life Coach under Martha Beck and Brooke Castillo's certification programs.

Kris is the corporate expert when it comes to taking the *Self-Coaching Model* into corporations and organizations through employee to management level coaching. She has assembled a highly regarded corporate coaching team and has utilized the *Self-Coaching Model* in numerous workshops.

Kris lives in Northern California with her husband of 15 years, three wonderful kids and her chocolate lab, Grizz.

You can learn more about Kris at www.krisplachy.com.